THE KING OF THE HILL

SPRING
HARVEST
Equipping the Church for action

Copyright©2001 Spring Harvest

Jeff Lucas asserts the moral right to be identified as the author of this work.

Published by
Spring Harvest
14 Horsted Square
Uckfield
East Sussex TN22 1QL

First edition 2001

Acknowledgements
Scripture quotations taken from the HOLY BIBLE, NEW INTERNATIONAL VERSION.
Copyright ©1973, 1978, 1984 by International Bible Society.
Used by permission of Hodder and Stoughton Limited.
All rights reserved.

"NIV" is a registered trade mark of International Bible Society.
UK trademark number 1448790

Thank you to Sunrise Software for the supply of Quickverse Bible Study software.

Please note that the inclusion of a quotation or example in this book does not imply endorsement by Spring Harvest.

Printed and bound in Malta.

Spring Harvest. A Registered Charity.

ISBN   1 899788 34 4

King
of the hill

Spring Harvest 2001
Study Guide

by Jeff Lucas

SPRING HARVEST
Equipping the Church for action

Using your Study Guide

At the beginning of each section is a BIBLE PASSAGE from Matthew's gospel with space for you to write some notes. Then there's a MENU – an overview of the material that follows.

Following is the MAIN COURSE – the body of the material itself. The MAIN COURSE is served up in two-page helpings, and is a resource centre. The left-hand page contains the main body of the teaching material, with relevant quotations and references in the left margin. Throughout the text the ▮▮ PAUSE BUTTON icon draws your attention to key questions raised by the teaching material.

LINKS on the right-hand page point to more information that amplifies or illustrates the teaching material.

RESOURCE LINKS
references to books, web sites or organizations.

A book.link [book link] is a pointer to a book you might like to read to study a particular issue in greater depth.

A Web.link [www] provides details of a web site or page on the internet where you can find further information.

FURTHER INFORMATION LINKS
more detailed material to complement the core teaching material.

A past.link [icon] is a historical link giving a perspective from history that illustrates the subject.

A plus.link [plus link] is more detail, perhaps a newspaper article or research paper that amplifies or comments on the material.

A theo.link [THEO LINK] contains more detailed theological or doctrinal material.

Introduction

This Spring Harvest Study Guide takes an in-depth look at the manifesto announced by Jesus at the start of his ministry. We call it the Sermon on the Mount and it can be found in Matthew's gospel, chapters 5, 6 and 7.

The King of the universe became the King of the hill – making known the values of his kingdom and teaching them in a way that was accessible to all. In our society, as it was 2000 years ago, these values clash with the culture and challenge us at every level. Our aim is to allow the radical words of Jesus to challenge and change us, our churches and our communities.

Contents

THE KING OF THE HILL

BIBLE PASSAGE

MATTHEW

5:1–12

[1]Now when he saw the crowds, he went up on a mountainside and sat down. His disciples came to him, [2]and he began to teach them, saying:

[3]"Blessed are the poor in spirit,
    for theirs is the kingdom of heaven.
[4]Blessed are those who mourn,
    for they will be comforted.
[5]Blessed are the meek,
    for they will inherit the earth.
[6]Blessed are those who hunger and thirst for righteousness,
    for they will be filled.
[7]Blessed are the merciful,
    for they will be shown mercy.
[8]Blessed are the pure in heart,
    for they will see God.
[9]Blessed are the peacemakers,
    for they will be called sons of God.
[10]Blessed are those who are persecuted because of righteousness,
    for theirs is the kingdom of heaven.

[11]"Blessed are you when people insult you, persecute you and falsely say all kinds of evil against you because of me. [12]Rejoice and be glad, because great is your reward in heaven, for in the same way they persecuted the prophets who were before you."

6:33

"But seek first his kingdom and his righteousness, and all these things will be given to you as well."

Today focuses on the passages above, but provides a 'helicoptic' view of Matthew Chapters 5 to 7.

NOTES

King
of the hill

NOTES

THE KING'S ARMS

THE KING'S ARMS – MENU

Before we delve into detail, we will take a look at the big picture. Who was Jesus addressing when he spoke? What are the big themes of the Sermon? Have we focused on the detail and missed the point?

We will be introduced to the radical nature of Jesus' message and the way he introduces a totally different way to live. There is a big welcome in the King's arms.

King of the hill

"... the Sermon on the Mount. ... engenders dreams of a better world. ... I have fallen under its spell, or rather under the spell of him who preached it."
– John Stott

"... the best sermon in the history of the world – the Sermon on the Mount."
– Stephen Gaukroger

"All the articles of our religion ... all the body of divinity, is in ... this one Sermon on the Mount."
– John Donne, Lent 1629

"The Sermon on the Mount ... is probably the best known part of the teaching of Jesus. ... arguably it is the least understood, and certainly it is the least obeyed."
– John Stott

"Nothing could be more thrilling to a Bible student than to devote time to the study of Jesus' Great Sermon. ... to drink in Jesus' teaching is to savour a foretaste of heaven."
– Rob Warner

"The Sermon on the Mount: the supreme jewel in the crown of Jesus' teaching."
– Michael Green

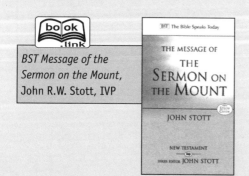

BST Message of the Sermon on the Mount, John R.W. Stott, IVP

The Way that Leads to Life, Michael Eaton, Christian Focus Publications

INTRODUCTION – THE FOURTEEN-MINUTE EPIC

The Sermon on the Mount. It's often called the Great Sermon. It takes around fourteen minutes to read aloud. It's been given incredible reviews: One writer calls it the "manifesto of Jesus;" a second calls it the "greatest, the most searching, the most challenging part of the Bible;" another says, "The Sermon on the Mount is the most important and controversial biblical text." Our study of the sermon is vital and relevant because it is here that Jesus answers the central question of the third millennium — how should we live?

Specifically, the Sermon on the Mount deals with vital questions such as:

● The Kingdom of God – what is it and why don't we hear more about it? (Matt 6:33)

● If the Christian community is to be like a city on a hill that cannot be hidden (Matt 5:14), then how should we be different from those without Christ?

● Is the church called to prioritise cultural relevance – or are we to seek, to use John Stott's phrase, "Christian counter-culture"? Or both? (Matt 5:13; Rom 12:1–2)

● Do we separate our lives into "sacred" and "secular" compartments?

● What is true righteousness? And if religious, pharisaic "righteousness" disgusts God (Matt 23:1–39) then what pleases him?

● Is there a conflict between evangelism and social action? (Matt 5:13–16)

● What should our attitude be to money, ambition and relationships? (Matt 5:38–48, 6:19–24, 7:1–6)

● How do we develop a life of friendship with God? What about prayer? Is discipline important? (Matt 6:5–18, 7:7–12)

● What action is God asking us to take – and are we better at believing than doing? Matt 7:24–27)

The place and the people

The teaching we know today as the Sermon on the Mount was delivered early in the public ministry of Jesus in Galilee, perhaps in early to mid AD31. Immediately after his baptism and temptation he began to announce the good news of the kingdom of God (Matt 4:23). Jesus was experiencing popularity with the masses – with the

THE KING'S ARMS

SERMON OR SERMONS?

Jesus never described his teaching as a sermon. Augustine of Hippo (354–430), the North African theologian, first used the title in his writings. Some scholars suggest that it was not a sermon delivered in one place and at one sitting at all – but rather a summary of the teaching of Jesus compiled by Matthew, acting as an editor. W.D. Davies calls the sermon 'a collection of unrelated sayings … a patchwork'. Calvin believed something similar: "a collection of the leading points of the doctrine of Christ which related to a holy and devout life."

However, Matthew puts the 'sermon' into a specific geographical and historical context, describing it as an event, using terms that mark the beginning and the conclusion of the teaching period (Matt 5:1, 7:28); See also Matt 11:1, 13:53, 19:1, 26:1). The teaching also has the 'shape' of a sermon, with an introduction, an overall theme, and a dramatic climax. A.W. Blackwood, the Princeton scholar, states the necessity of reading the Sermon on the Mount as a sermon – it has "a masterful unity." Martyn Lloyd-Jones calls the sermon "a symphony".

Michael Eaton rejects the idea of Matthew as compiling editor, but does "not find it necessary to think that it was one 'sermon'. More likely, Matthew 5–7 is an abridged statement of the teaching that Jesus gave during an entire day or over the course of several days. It is obviously a summary." Commentators such as John Stott and A.B. Bruce agree with this approach.

BIRD'S EYE VIEW

So, where is the hill up which Jesus climbed to deliver his message? Although tradition has identified it with Karn Hattin, near Capernaum, its exact location is unknown.

WHO WAS JESUS SPEAKING TO?

Two words are used to describe the group that gathered to hear Jesus' teaching – *crowd* and *disciples*. This is interpreted by some to indicate that the specifically chosen inner circle of disciples would have been closest to Jesus, and therefore able to listen to the detail of every word he taught, and that there would have been a larger, scattered group spread out across the hillside. Also, the word 'disciple' does not need only to refer to the twelve but could be used to describe many of the crowd on that occasion, because they listened as pupils or learners do.

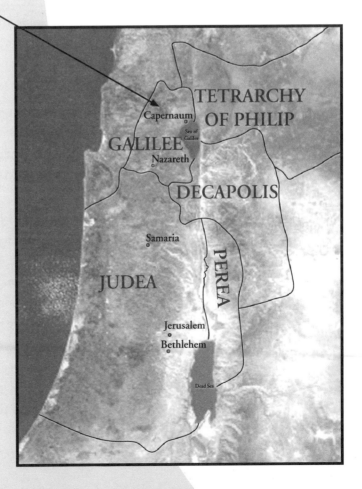

King of the hill

"The Sermon ... is not so much ethics of obedience as ethics of grace."

– Amos Wilder

"People in the first century who heard this teaching of Jesus were living under enormous stress. Israel at that time was like one big pressure cooker."

– Stephen Gaukroger

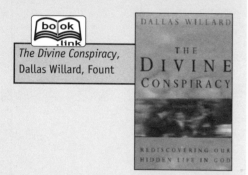

The Divine Conspiracy, Dallas Willard, Fount

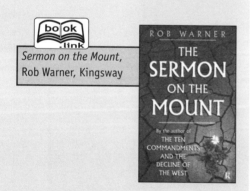

Sermon on the Mount, Rob Warner, Kingsway

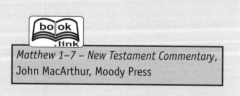

Matthew 1–7 – New Testament Commentary, John MacArthur, Moody Press

Studies in the Sermon on the Mount, D. Martyn Lloyd-Jones, IVP

notable exception of the Pharisees (Mark 3:6; Luke 6:11). Crowds were being drawn from as far away as Idumea, 100 miles to the south, and from Tyre and Sidon some 50 miles north (Mark 3:7–12). Many were attracted by the miracles. It was time to teach them about the kingdom of God: the King of kings climbed a hill to deliver that message.

A hillside near Capernaum that sweeps up gently from the Sea of Galilee was the location for this teaching session. It was an area Jesus often used for private prayer retreats. Some commentators make much of the fact that Jesus 'went up the mountain' in the same way that Moses went up a mountain to receive the law (Exod 19:20). But Jesus climbs the mountain not to receive the words, but to declare and teach them.

A sermon with a purpose

The context and purpose of the Sermon in Matthew's Gospel is that Jesus stood before a downtrodden, oppressed people, who were living under the heel of Roman occupation. Some were violent, anti-Roman zealots whose motto was 'Let their blood be spilled on the streets'. Some were escapists – like the Essenes, who fled from the corruption of community life and established their own base in the desert. Some were compromisers – like Matthew himself, a tax gatherer for the hated Romans. Others – the majority – just surrendered themselves to the situation, probably feeling there was nothing that could be done. There was no other way to live.

The King stood on a hill to announce that they were wrong. A new kingdom – the sphere of God's rule and reign, a new world order – was breaking into their lives. Matthew's Gospel sets this out as follows:

- Section 1: Matt 1:1–4:16 Jesus' identity is established, particularly from the teaching of the Old Testament.
- Section 2: Matt 4:17–16:20 Jesus fulfils the kingly authority of God's kingdom in his teaching, in his deeds of grace and power, and his summons to enter the kingdom of God.
- Section 3: Matt 16:21-28:20 Jesus is the suffering king who is crucified, but conquers death and sends his messengers out into the world to bring all nations into his kingdom. All authority in heaven and on earth is his (Matt 28:18). His is the kingdom and the power and the glory forever.

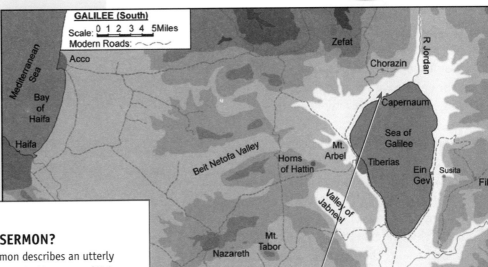

WHAT IS THE PURPOSE OF THE SERMON?

Even a glance will show us that the sermon describes an utterly radical – and therefore some suggest unattainable – way of living. Harvey McArthur in "Understanding the Sermon on the Mount" suggests at least twelve different ways of interpreting the Sermon. Clarence Bauman lists 19. Among these are that the Sermon is:

- **A welcoming call**, an invitation of grace to the poor and those who mourn, to enjoy the royal reign of God's love in Christ. Dallas Willard puts this view forward in his book "The Divine Conspiracy".

- **A mirror of perfection** to show us our need. Just as the law is a school teacher that shows us our need of God, so the lofty ethical statements of the Sermon drive us back to our need of salvation. Martin Dibelius saw the Great Sermon as a spelling out of "the will of God, however unreachable." G.K. Chesterton said of the Sermon on the Mount, "This is impossible stuff!"

- **A pattern to build a new society**. The view espoused by Tolstoy, which if obeyed literally would "do away with existing evils and usher in a Utopian Kingdom". Tolstoy distilled the Sermon into five tenets: suppression of anger, no oaths, non-resistance, unreserved love of enemies, and chastity.

- **The new law of Jesus**. By far the greatest temptation to Christians is to interpret the Sermon as a set of legalised commandments that are, to quote Sir John Seeley, "Christ's legislation". Augustine was among the first to espouse this approach.

- **An interim ethic**. Popularised by Weiss and Schweitzer, the Sermon was an ethical system for use during Jesus' earthly life and is no longer appropriate for the new age, which has been ushered in by his death and resurrection.

- **A standard for the 'spiritually elite'**. A subtle form of this idea would definitely exist among some Christians. Some of the early monastic communities embraced this view.

- **A description of an age to come**. The well worn dispensational view would again find some sympathy among those Christians feeling intimidated by what they see as the demands of the Sermon and feeling that it can only really be lived after Christ has returned – which is very difficult to reconcile when you consider comments about persecution.

The Church of the Beatitudes, traditionally the site of the Sermon on the Mount, looks out over the Sea of Galilee from a hillside near Capernaum.

King
of the hill

"I did as I was told. I was fussy about my peanut butter, fought cavities, became depressed over yellow wax buildup. ... I was responsible for my husband's underarms being protected for twelve hours. I alone was carrying the burden for my dog's shiny coat. We believed if we converted all the products that marched before our eyes we could be the best, the sexiest, the freshest, the cleanest, the thinnest, the smartest and the first in our block to be regular. Purchasing for the whole family was the most important thing I had to do."
– Erma Bombeck

"We don't know how to be the church, because we don't quite know how we are supposed to live in the world."
– Mike Regele

Why Settle for More & Miss the Best?, Tom Sine, Word

The Goldsworthy Trilogy, Graeme Goldsworthy, Paternoster

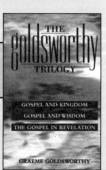

Gospel of the Kingdom, George Eldon Ladd, Eerdmans

Pause button
Over the next few days, we are going to ask some searching questions about the way we live. Our circumstances are different from those of the crowd that gathered 2000 years ago in the foothills of Galilee to hear the Great Sermon. But like theirs, our lives can be pressure cookers of stress, misplaced values, and meaninglessness. To quote Tom Sine, "We seem to dance to someone else's tune and never question the melody." Pause for a moment now and pray a huge prayer: "Father, show me how to live."

THE HEARTBEAT OF THE SERMON

When Jesus sat down to preach the Great Sermon, he was addressing a crowd of 'kingdom-less' people. They had no land to call their own – it was occupied by the Romans.

Jesus' life message was about another kingdom – not a land or a nation, but rather the kingdom of God. The word kingdom means "range of effective will or rule". This kingdom did not begin with Christ's incarnation; the kingdom of God is eternal and, in terms of human history, is pictured in the Garden of Eden. The news of the kingdom of God coming among women and men was at the very heart of the teaching of Jesus. It was his prime concern, his central theme.

- He called people to, "Repent, for the kingdom of heaven is near." – Matt 4:17
- He taught on how to enter the kingdom – Matt 5:20, 7:21
- His miracles were signs of the kingdom – Matt 12:28
- His parables provided insights and truth about kingdom life – Matt 13:11
- He taught his followers to pray "your kingdom come" – Matt 6:10
- The heartbeat of the Sermon on the Mount is the call to "seek first his kingdom" – Matt 6:33

WHICH MOUNT ARE YOU CLIMBING?

There's a story called Hope for the Flowers. It's about an ambitious caterpillar named Stripe who decided to climb a mountain made of caterpillars, all climbing over each other, trying to get to the top. As Stripe plunged into the pile and began his ascent, he asked, "What's at the top?" Another climber responded, "No one knows, but it must be awfully good because everyone's rushing there..."

Stripe soon found that moving up the mountain was a struggle. He was pushed and kicked and stepped on from every direction. It was climb or be climbed. But Stripe disciplined himself neither to feel or be distracted as he continued to push his way up. "Don't blame me if you don't succeed! It's a tough life. Just make up your mind", he yelled to any complainers.

Finally, Stripe neared to the top of the humongous mountain of caterpillars. As he looked ahead, he saw something disturbing: a tremendous pressure and shaking was sending many at the top crashing to their death below. Stripe felt awful with this new knowledge. The mystery of the pillar was clearing. He now knew what always must happen on the pillar. Frustration surged through Stripe. But as he agreed this was the only way 'up' he heard a tiny whisper from the top. "There's nothing here at all!" It was answered by another: "Quiet, fool! They'll hear you down the pillar. We're where they want to be. That's what's here."

Stripe felt frozen. To be so high and not be high at all. It only looked good from the bottom.

– *Tom Sine,* Why settle for more and miss the best?

GARDEN OF EDEN

Jesus did not announce the "launch" of God's kingdom – which has been in existence eternally, since God's reign and rule is eternal. Eden is a picture of the kingdom; the Creator and his creation in ruler-and-subject relationship. The "garden kingdom" shows us a picture of:

▶ God's people (Adam and Eve)
▶ In God's place (the Garden of Eden)
▶ Under God's rule (the word of God).

King *of the hill*

"The kingdom creates the church, works through the church and is proclaimed in the world by the church. There can be no kingdom without a church (those who have acknowledged God's rule) and there can be no church without God's kingdom; but they remain two distinguishable concepts – the rule of God and the fellowship of men."

– George Eldon Ladd

"I cannot help wondering out loud why I haven't heard more about the kingdom in the thirty years I have been a Christian. I certainly read about it enough in the Bible ... but I honestly cannot remember any pastor whose ministry I have been under actually preaching a sermon on the kingdom of God. As I rummage through my own sermon barrel, I now realize that I myself have never preached a sermon on it. Where has the kingdom been?"

– C. Peter Wagner

"During the past sixteen years I can recollect only two occasions on which I have heard sermons specifically devoted to the theme of the kingdom of God. ... I find this silence rather surprising because it is universally agreed by New Testament scholars that the central theme of the teaching of Jesus was the kingdom of God."

– Dr. I. Howard Marshall (University of Aberdeen)

The surprising silence

Considering the central and primary emphasis Jesus places upon the kingdom, we could expect it to be a central part of the message of the Christian church. This is not the case. Perhaps we have forgotten the kingdom – the very core of the message of Jesus.

At the Lausanne Conference in 1974, Michael Green asked rhetorically: "How much have you heard about the kingdom of God?" His answer was: "Not much. It is not our language. But it was Jesus' prime concern."

Perhaps the silence is due in part to the fact that the kingdom of God is an abstract concept that is difficult to comprehend – we are used to thinking about kingdoms that relate to specific nations and geographical areas, for example the United Kingdom. Couple this with another challenge to our Western logic: the Bible teaches that the kingdom of God is both *now* and *yet to come*.

Now and not yet

● The kingdom is NOW. It's already here. (Rom 14:17; Col 1:13; Luke 17.20–21; Matt 21.31). But some take the view that the kingdom is entirely to be established in the here and now – it's about earth. This view places aside the future – apocalyptic – promises of the final consummation of the kingdom becoming a reality only when Christ returns.

● The kingdom is YET TO COME. It's not yet complete. (Luke 22:22–30; Matt 25:31-34; 2 Peter 1:11; Mark 9:47). But some take the view that the kingdom is entirely in the future – it's about heaven. Matthew's use of the term 'kingdom of heaven' 32 times does not indicate that the kingdom is a futuristic, other-worldly one. It is simply an expression of his Jewishness, shown in his reluctance to over-use the word 'God'

● So we live between the ages – 1 Cor 10:11

● We have tasted the powers of the coming age – Heb 6:5

● We live between the already and the not yet. We have the down payment, the guarantee – but there is more to come – Eph 1:13,14

● We are still to enter the kingdom – and we must do so through 'many trials' – Acts 14:22

● The kingdom comes in the person of Jesus – Luke 11:20, 17:20

● The kingdom comes as it is received – Matt 6:33.

THE KING'S ARMS

THE KINGDOM

The vocabulary of the kingdom is continually on Jesus' lips. Most biblical scholars do agree that the "kingdom of God" means the dynamic rule or reign of God. The reign of God represents God's government, authority and ruling power. It isn't a territory in a spatial sense. The kingdom doesn't stand on a particular piece of ground. Nor is it static. It's dynamic – always becoming, spreading, and growing. The kingdom is present whenever and wherever women and men submit their lives to God's authority.

Does the kingdom occur when God rules in the hearts of people? This notion suggests that the kingdom is primarily an internal, inward experience of the mind. But the very term 'kingdom' implies a collective order above and beyond the experience of any one person. A kingdom in a literal sense means that a king rules over a group of people. Social standards and group policies order the collective life of a kingdom. Agreements spell out citizens' obligations to each other as well as to their king. The king's ruling activity makes practical differences in the lives and relationships of his subjects. In the words of one scholar, "The kingdom is something people enter, not something that enters them. It is a state of affairs, not a state of mind".

Kingdom living is fundamentally social. It involves membership, citizenship, loyalties, and one's identity. Citizenship in a kingdom entails relationships, policies, obligations, boundaries and expectations. These dimensions of kingdom life supersede the whims of individual experience. Membership in a kingdom spells out a citizen's relationship to the king, to other citizens, and to other kingdoms. Living in a kingdom means sharing in its history and helping to shape its future.

The kingdom of God is a collectivity – a network of persons who have yielded their hearts and relationships to the reign of God. The kingdom is actualized when God rules in hearts and social relationships. The kingdom isn't merely a series of independent spiritual fax lines linking the King to each subject. The reign of God infuses the web of relationships, binding King and citizens together.

How do we discover what God's reign looks like? What is the shape of the royal policies? Can we translate the lofty idea of God's reign into practical terms? The answer lies in the incarnation. Jesus of Nazareth unveiled God. We begin to grasp the meaning of the kingdom through Jesus' life and teachings. The life, death and resurrection of Jesus was God's final and definitive word. Through Jesus' person and ministry, God's voice clearly spoke, in a universal language understood by all.

– Adapted from The Upside Down Kingdom, *Donald B. Kraybill*

NOW AND YET TO COME

"Some who are inspired by a utopian vision seem to suggest that God's kingdom, in all its fullness, can be built on earth. We do not subscribe to this view since Scripture informs us of the reality and pervasiveness of both personal and societal sin ...

"Other Christians are tempted to turn their eyes away from this world and fix them so exclusively on the return of Christ that their involvement in the here and now is paralysed. We do not endorse this view either, since it denies the biblical injunctions to defend the cause of the weak, maintain the rights of the poor and oppressed (Psa 82:3) and practice justice and love (Micah 6:8).

"We affirm that the kingdom of God is both present and future, both societal and individual, both physical and spiritual."

– The Wheaton Declaration of 1983

King of the hill

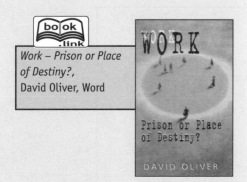

book.link

Work – Prison or Place of Destiny?, David Oliver, Word

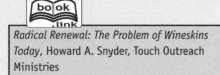

book.link

Radical Renewal: The Problem of Wineskins Today, Howard A. Snyder, Touch Outreach Ministries

> "Jesus' good news then, was that the kingdom of God had come, and that he, Jesus, was its herald and expounder to men. More than that, in some special, mysterious way, he was the kingdom."
>
> – Malcolm Muggeridge

> "The church gets into trouble whenever it thinks it is in the church business rather than the kingdom business. In the church business people are concerned with church activities, religious behaviour and spiritual things. In the kingdom business, people are concerned with kingdom activities, all human behaviour and everything which God has made, visible and invisible. Church people think how to get people into the church, kingdom people think about how to get the church into the world. Church people worry that the world might change the church, kingdom people work to see the church change the world!"
>
> – Howard Snyder, Liberating the church

Heartbeat or murmur?

Does all this really matter? Is this just an issue for the theologians? Should we concern ourselves about this 'kingdom' message at all?

It matters a great deal, if we are to be:

● **Faithful to Scripture**. The kingdom is so central to both Old and New Testaments, so fundamental to the preaching of Jesus, that we must recover kingdom centrality. We need a kingdom consciousness – an awareness of the kingdom of God – that is biblically based.

● **People of biblical lifestyle**. We will see in this section that the truth of the kingdom makes radical demands on every area of our lives. Without the message of the kingdom, we too easily fall into the idea that God is interested only in church activity, and is really at work only within the church. This leads us into the thoroughly unbiblical 'sacred and secular' thinking that is prevalent in the church. Mark Greene of the London Institute for Contemporary Christianity recently said: 'This sacred/secular divide remains one of the greatest challenges to the effectiveness of the church.'

● **Clear in the message** of the gospel, which is 'the gospel of the kingdom'. Our message is not an offer of sin management in the here and now, with the hope of the rule of God reserved for the future. It is not a call to 'invite Jesus to come into your heart' – but rather an invitation to everyone to step into his kingdom in the here and now (Matt 5:20, 18:3; John 3:3,5). If everything is locked in the future, then Christianity becomes a death cult. Our message will have little relevance to young people, for whom death is often a far distant, unfathomable concept.

● **Live a God-centred life**. Familiar as we are with the call to "seek first his kingdom" (Matt 6:33), in reality we often view the church as something that exists for us rather than as an agent for the extension of God's kingdom. A kingdom mentality realises that the church is not there to serve us; its structures and programmes are temporary, and therefore we should be flexible in our approach to them. The now-but-not-yet tension of the kingdom calls us to patience with the church corporately and with one another individually. We are not yet fully what we shall be – we are all a work in progress, awaiting the final completion and consummation.

THE KING'S ARMS

THE ALREADY BUT NOT YET

Oscar Cullmann uses the illustration of D-Day and VE Day. Most agree that victory was guaranteed in World War II when the allies landed in Normandy (June 6, 1944). Victory was inevitable but not yet realized until VE Day, which took place 11 months later. Or even VJ Day on 2 September, 1945, when Japan surrendered.

"Historically, the people of God have disagreed not so much over what God is doing in the world but over when he will do it. Most Christians admit that, in one sense or other, God is bringing history to a cosmic climax. But one branch has said 'Not now: then!' And, in reaction, another group has said 'Not then: now!' Those who postpone any real presence of the kingdom until after Christ's return (Not now: then) do not expect any substantial renewal now except in the realm of individual human experience – not in politics, art, education, culture in general, and not even, really, in the church. On the other side are those who so emphasize present renewal in society in general that both personal conversion and space-time future return of Christ are denied and overshadowed, and man's deep sinfulness is not taken seriously.

"Hopefully, Christians today ... are coming to see that the kingdom of God is neither entirely present nor entirely future. The kingdom of God ... is now here, is coming and will come."

– Howard Snyder

KINGDOM OF HEAVEN

Matthew uses the terms 'kingdom of heaven' and 'kingdom of God (Matt 19:23–24) synonymously. This does not suggest two kingdoms: Matthew records Jesus saying that the secrets of the *kingdom of heaven* had been given to his disciples (Matt 13:11) whereas Mark describes the same conversation using the phrase the secret of the *kingdom of God* (Mark 4:11).

In Matthew, Jesus says the *kingdom of heaven* belongs to such as little children (Matt 19:14), while Mark quotes him as saying *kingdom of God* (Mark 10:14). Most commentators agree that this is simply because Matthew, writing for a Jewish audience, would have been hesitant to use the phrase 'of God', because the rabbis were concerned not to use the word 'god' in case they misused it in any way. Other terms are used to describe the same kingdom in the New Testament – "kingdom of Christ and of God" (Eph 5:5) and "kingdom of light" (Col 1:12).

The use of 'kingdom' arises from a similar Jewish concern. The rabbis disliked using verbs of God. For example, the Targum of Onkelos translates 'the Lord shall reign' (Ex 15:18) as 'God's kingly rule'. A dynamic phrase about God's activity is replaced by a static one.

KINGDOM PEOPLE

"Kingdom people seek first the kingdom of God and its justice. Church people often put church work above work, above concerns of justice, mercy and truth. Church people think about how to get people into the church and that is probably why our evangelism is by and large ineffectual. ...

"Church people don't usually like parties, alcohol or bad people. The King of the kingdom liked all three. When Christians put the church ahead of the kingdom, they settle for meetings and they spend increasing amounts of time with the same people. When they catch a vision of the kingdom of God, their sight shifts to the poor, the orphan, the widow, the refugee, the wretched of the earth and to God's future. They also see with real insight and fresh vision the stressed, the fearful, the hopeless at work and both their heart and their time reach out. If the church has one great need, it is this – to be set free, for the kingdom of God, to be set free from the second wave and to become relevant exactly as God intended."

– David Oliver, Work – Prison or Place of Destiny?

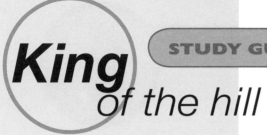

King
of the hill

The Trivialisation of God,
Donald McCullough, Navpress

The Community of the King,
Howard A. Snyder, IVP-US

"The kingdom is something people enter, not something that enters them."

– Allen Verhey

"Would anyone, by summoning all powers of thought and imagination, have dreamed of a God born not in the presence of kings but of barnyard animals, a God mewling and messing diapers, a God wandering around a backwater province of the Roman Empire with an inconsequential band of followers, a God performing a few mighty miracles in the presence of much suffering, a God rejected by pastors and theologians and the most pious of the land, a God charged with blasphemy and nailed to die on a cross? Who could have imagined this to be a representation of God?"

– Donald McCullough

THE RADICAL CALL OF THE SERMON

Everything is different

Jesus' radical heartbeat can be sensed in every word of the Sermon on the Mount. This is not a quiet, devotional homily, but an explosive call to dynamic living. Those hearing Jesus preach the sermon were shocked and astounded at his words. Our familiarity with them can blunt their cutting edge. And this is not just a radical presentation – the King himself embodies the most shocking, surprising behaviour.

The core of the sermon is a call for God's people to be entirely different. One writer identifies the key text of the sermon to be Matt 6:8 "Do not be like them," a cry later picked up by Paul when he urges "Do not conform" (Rom 12:2). Just as the call to Israel was "You must not do as they do" (Lev 18:3), the distinct character of the people of God is a theme continuously reiterated by the King of the Hill.

Like lights set on stands (Matt 5:14) and like flavourful salt (Matt 5:13) so the children of God are not to take their cue from the people around them but from God, and be known by their utterly radical lifestyle. In the Old Testament, God's people are constantly getting into trouble because they long to be like those around them (Num 23:9; Psa 106:35; 1 Sam 8:5,19,20; Ezek 20:32).

Jesus calls his followers to be different from:
● The scribes and the Pharisees (Matt 5:20)
● Their 'pagan' neighbours, the Gentiles (Matt 6:7,32)
● Their fellow Jews (Matt 6:5,16)

Examples of this different behaviour are everywhere in the sermon:
● Some people love and salute each other, but followers of Jesus love their enemies (Matt 5:44–47)
● Some people pray empty prayers, but followers of Jesus draw near to the Father with intimacy (Matt 6:7–13)
● Some people are preoccupied with materialism and 'success,' but followers of Jesus are primarily concerned with God's rule and righteousness (Matt 6:32,33)

THE KING'S ARMS

JESUS CALLED HIS FOLLOWERS TO BE DIFFERENT

Blessed are the wealthy, because theirs is the Dow Jones index.

Blessed are those who enjoy a good party, because they will drown their sorrows.

Blessed are the assertive, for they will get to the top of their career.

Blessed are those who hunger and thirst after chemical stimulation, for designer
    drugs are more widely available with every passing year.

Blessed are the ruthless, because no one will get in their way.

Blessed are the cold of heart, for they won't get hurt when relationships break
    down.

Blessed are those who are involved in the arms trade, for theirs are the best deals
    in developing nations.

Blessed are the directors of privatised utilities, for theirs are the fat cat bonuses.

– created by Spring Harvest guests, 1997, compiled by Rob Warner

A CONTEMPORARY RELEVANT CALL

Kingdom social ethics, taught and lived by Jesus, can be transported over the bridge linking the first and twenty-first centuries. The Gospels don't offer a full-blown system of formal ethics to cover every conceivable situation. I don't espouse a sentimentalist mentality of simply 'walking in his footsteps.' But the Gospels do provide us with episodes, stories and pictures rife with insights applicable to our modern situation. The pictures of the good and the right lodged in the kingdom stories aren't impossible possibilities or romanticized ideals. They intersect at ground level with the knotty problems of human existence today.

The kingdom vision outlined in the Gospels doesn't spell out a specific programme for social ethics or political action. The New Testament vision does, however, clearly tell us what the kingdom is not. It also introduces us to the right and the good that undergird the kingdom. The specific applications, of course, are the work of the church – over the centuries – as directed by the Holy Spirit.

God enjoins us to enter [the kingdom]. God calls us to turn our backs on the kingdoms of this world and embrace an upside-down home. Underlying all Jesus' teaching about the kingdom is a call to respond. He invites us not to study but to join; not to dissect but to enter. How will we respond?

– Donald B. Kraybill

King
of the hill

"The Sermon on the Mount is the most complete delineation anywhere in the New Testament of the Christian counter-culture. Here is a Christian value system, ethical standard, religious devotion, attitude to money, ambition, life-style and network of relationships – all of which are totally at variance with those of the non-Christian world. And this Christian counter-culture is the life of the kingdom of God, a fully human life indeed but lived out under the divine rule."

– John Stott

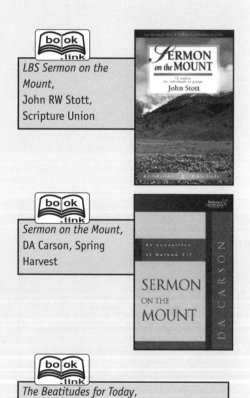

book link
LBS Sermon on the Mount,
John RW Stott,
Scripture Union

book link
Sermon on the Mount,
DA Carson, Spring
Harvest

book link
The Beatitudes for Today,
John Blanchard, Day One

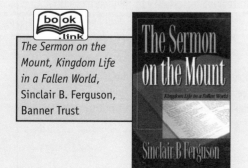

book link
The Sermon on the Mount, Kingdom Life in a Fallen World,
Sinclair B. Ferguson,
Banner Trust

The call to be different is not only for those who heard these words from the lips of Jesus 2000 years ago. It is a contemporary, relevant call for us too with all of our Third Millennium challenges and opportunities.

Radical examples

Some of the greatest examples of the call to be different are found in the Beatitudes (Matt 5:3–12). Scholars have endlessly debated the Beatitudes. Are they a description of Christian character and a portrayal of kingdom life, or a welcome and a promise of "blessedness" to the downtrodden and oppressed?

Perhaps they are both. Certainly the Beatitudes do not teach salvation by attitude, but they do give us a sense of the radical kingdom lifestyle Jesus calls us to. It is as if Jesus has crept into the window display of life and changed the price tags. It's all upside down. The first three statements Jesus makes illustrate this radical 'upside-down' value system.

> In a world where 'success' and 'self-sufficiency' are applauded, and 'the beautiful people' are ambitious, accomplished and wealthy, Jesus teaches:

Blessed are the poor in spirit (Matt 5:3)

Jesus is not talking about a financial or a depressive condition, about bad self image or morbidity. Blessed are those who feel their own emptiness, he says, who are conscious of their weakness, who call out in desperation to God, like the tax collector: "God, have mercy on me, a sinner" (Luke 18:13). Those who confidently assume they have 'the spiritual goods' are most likely wrong.

The church of England's General Confession says, "… there is no health in us." Those who recognise in this way that they have nothing are judged to be really 'well off'. The kingdom of heaven is theirs.

> Our culture encourages us to discard guilt and the sorrow that accompanies pangs of conscience. Happiness is everything, entertainment is king. Jesus teaches:

Blessed are those who mourn (v4)

Jesus is not hostile to fun or laughter. He does not call us to a perpetual state of sadness. Rather he tells us that those who acknowl-

SALVATION BY ATTITUDE

God does not bless us because of any good works we do – only because of the finished work of Christ on the cross. The person who says "I just try to live out the Sermon on the Mount" has not understood the heart of the sermon at all. Only those cleansed by the blood of Christ, filled with the Holy Spirit, and instructed by God's Word can begin to walk in this kingdom lifestyle. (Rom 3:23; Gal 3:10, 24; Eph 2:8–9). As Martin Lloyd Jones puts it: "There is nothing that so leads to the gospel and its grace as the Sermon on the Mount." We are not saved by keeping the teaching of the sermon.

Martin Luther says: "Christ is saying nothing in this sermon about how we become Christians, but only about the works and fruit that no one can do unless he is already a Christian and in a state of grace."

John Blanchard says: "There is no indication in the Sermon on the Mount that obeying the 'Golden Rule' is the way of salvation. ... if the ability to keep the rules were to be treated as a test to gain salvation no-one would ever pass the test. The whole idea that they might is smashed to smithereens by the Bible's insistence that "all have sinned and fall short of the glory of God" (Rom 3:23). Nobody keeps the golden rule, or even comes close to doing so. What is more, all who hope that their attempts to do so might be acceptable are faced with an uncompromising fact: "All who rely on observing the law are under a curse, for it is written: 'Cursed is everyone who does not continue to do everything written in the Book of the Law.'" (Gal 3:10) Notice the word 'everything'. Any attempt to gain salvation by morality or religion is an exercise in futility.

"It is implicit in the Sermon on the Mount and explicit elsewhere in Scripture that salvation is entirely by the grace of God. As Paul wrote to the Christians of his day, 'For it is by grace you have been saved, through faith – and this not from yourselves, it is the gift of God – not by works, so that no-one can boast.' (Eph 2:8–9) "

– John Blanchard

POOR IN SPIRIT

In the Old Testament 'the poor' is a technical term for a particular group of people. Psa 34:6 talks of "this poor man" who called on the Lord and was heard and saved. In Psa 40:17, the author describes himself as "poor and needy" and asks the Lord to remember him and deliver him ... the poor are the needy and the captives who seek God as their only refuge and salvation (Psa 69:32–33). They are the bankrupt of this world, who know themselves to be so, and who therefore trust in the Lord as their only hope of protection and deliverance. ... we are urged today to develop almost every other kind of spirit except poverty of spirit. But the lack of this spirit can lead to spiritual ruin, as Jesus warned the Laodicean church: "You say, 'I am rich... '. But you do not realise that you are wretched, pitiful, poor, blind and naked." (Rev 3:17) If you would be rich and possess a kingdom, you must first lose all – including yourself and your self-centeredness – and become poor in spirit.

– Sinclair B. Ferguson

WHO IS REALLY WELL OFF?

Charles Spurgeon preached: "Do not come to him because you are fit – but because you are unfit to come. Your unfitness is your fitness. Your qualification is your lack of qualification." The Pharisees in Jesus' day thought themselves to be spiritually rich; the Zealots felt that they had the power to overcome their oppressors: but it was the weak, the dispossessed, the powerless 'sinners' who cried out to God for help – and were assured of his help.

King of the hill

"There is no single paragraph of the Sermon on the Mount in which the contrast between Christian and non-Christian standards is not drawn. It is the underlying and uniting theme of the Sermon – everything else is a variation of it."

– J.I. Packer

"Truly this is a new people, and there is something divine in them."

– Aristedes to the Emperor Hadrian, writing about 2ⁿᵈ century Christians

"In themselves, believers have no life, or strength, or spiritual power. All that they have of vital religion comes from Christ. They are what they are, and feel what they feel, and do what they do, because they draw out of Jesus a continual supply of grace, help and ability. Joined to the Lord by faith, and united in mysterious union with him by the Spirit, they stand, and walk, and continue, and run the Christian race. But every jot of good about them is drawn from their spiritual head, Jesus Christ."

– J.C. Ryle, Bishop of Liverpool

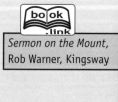

Sermon on the Mount, Rob Warner, Kingsway

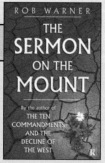

edge their lack (poverty of spirit) will grieve over their sinfulness and experience 'Godly sorrow' (Matt 26:75; 2 Cor 7:10). God draws close with comfort to those who take their sinfulness seriously (Psa 34:18, 40:1–3; Isa 61:1–3).

> In a competitive world, self-help seminars teach assertiveness and power is to be sought and used. Jesus teaches:

Blessed are the meek (v5)

Jesus calls on his followers to tame their tempers, living not out of control but under God's control. Meekness is not apathy, but willing adoption of a servant heart. Gentleness is celebrated in Scripture (Isa 53:7; John 13:5; Phil 4:5). In the kingdom of God, the way up is down.

Pause button

Some time today, take a few minutes out to reflect on the challenging words of Jesus in the Beatitudes (Matt 5:3–12) and what they mean for you in practical terms. Picture yourself sitting on the hillside with Jesus as he sets out the manifesto of his upside-down kingdom.

THE KING'S ARMS – EXTENDED TO RULE

Every area of life is affected

As we journey together this week, we shall see that Jesus calls us to a different kind of living – one that affects every area of our life. Some writers call it "whole life discipleship". *Is there such a thing as 'part life' discipleship?*

Three traps await us, each of which could deceive us into embracing something less than real discipleship:

Trap 1: Easy-believism

It's frequently said that Jesus gave the church the command to make disciples, not converts (Matt 28:19). It is possible to develop

THOSE WHO MOURN

The more clearly we see our own character – our instinctive bias to selfishness and impurity ... the more likely we are to enter into an experience of mourning over sin. This mourning is not reserved for the exceptionally wicked; it can find a valid and valuable experience in the life of every believer.

– Rob Warner

Those who mourn are those who care about their own wretched condition and care about a world bereft of the blessing of God.

– Frank Green

MARTIN LUTHER

Some commentators (like Hans Windisch, *The Meaning of the Sermon of the Mount*, 1929) have suggested that the words of the sermon are law that conflicts with Paul's gospel of grace. To quote Windisch: "From the standpoint of Paul, Luther and Calvin, the soteriology of the Sermon on the Mount is irredeemably heretical. [So,] there is a gulf here between Jesus and Paul that no art of theological exegesis can bridge."

Luther himself would have violently disagreed with this argument. The idea of salvation by some new form of law created 'hot indignation' in the reformer. He rebuked proponents of this idea as "those silly false preachers who have drawn the conclusion that we enter the kingdom of heaven and are saved by our own works and actions." He argued that such an idea "amounts to throwing the roof to the ground, upsetting the foundation, building salvation on mere water, hurling Christ from his throne completely and putting our works in his place." Evidently Luther shared the Pauline characteristic of being aggressive about people who teach salvation by works or law keeping (Gal 5:12), where Paul gently exhorts those of the circumcision party to go ahead and castrate themselves.

THE MEEK

These meek people inherit the earth. One would have expected the opposite. One would think that 'meek' people get nowhere because everybody ignores them or else rides roughshod over them and tramples them underfoot. It is the tough, the overbearing who succeed in the struggle for existence; weaklings go to the wall. Even the children of Israel had to fight for their inheritance, although the Lord God gave them the promised land. But the condition on which we enter our spiritual inheritance in Christ is not might but meekness, for ... everything is ours if we are Christ's (1 Cor 3:22). Psa 37, which Jesus seems to be quoting in the Beatitudes, says: "Do not fret because of evil men... . But the meek will inherit the land ... . Wait for the Lord and keep his way. He will exalt you to inherit the land; when the wicked are cut off, you will see it." The meek, although they may be deprived and disenfranchised by men, because they know what it is to live and reign with Christ, can enjoy and even 'possess' the earth, which belongs to Christ. Then on the day of 'the renewal' there will be 'a new heaven and a new earth' for them to inherit (Matt 19:28; 2 Pet 3:13; Rev 21:1). Thus the Christian even if he is like Paul in 'having nothing' can yet describe himself as 'possessing everything.' (2 Cor 6:10)

– John Stott

King
of the hill

"Jesus startles us. ... good guys turn out to be bad guys. Those we expect to receive the reward get a spanking instead. Those who think they are headed for heaven land in hell. Paradox, irony and surprise permeate the teachings of Jesus. They flip our expectations upside down. The least are the greatest. The immoral receive forgiveness and blessing. Adults become like children. The religious miss the heavenly banquet. The pious receive curses. Things aren't like we think they should be. We're baffled and perplexed. Amazed, we step back. Should we laugh or should we cry? Again and again, turning our world upside down, the kingdom surprises us."

– Donald Kraybill, The Upside Down Kingdom

"He only who is reduced to nothing in himself, and relies on the mercy of God, is poor in spirit."

– John Calvin

"In my morning devotions my soul was exceedingly melted, and bitterly mourned over my exceeding sinfulness and vileness."

– David Brainerd, journal entry for 18 October, 1740

"Sin must have tears."

– Thomas Watson

The Gospel According to Matthew, Leon Morris, IVP

---

salvation insurance, however, where people are invited to simply "ask Jesus into your heart" without seriously considering what it means to follow him daily. The implication is clear: If a person prays a 'sinners prayer' and believes the right things about God, that is sufficient.

Dietrich Bonhoeffer calls this approach 'cheap grace.' Jesus becomes comforter, forgiver and bringer of eternal life, but not the challenging King of the Hill who wants to be king of our lives. People caught in this trap view discipleship as an option for would-be martyrs, high profile clergy and overseas missionaries.

Consider these challenging words from Orlando Costas:

"Some people have a Christianity that is about an other-worldly kingdom, a privately inwardly limited spirit, a pocket God, a spiritualised Bible, and an escapist church. Such a Gospel makes possible the 'conversion' of men and women without having to make any drastic change in their lifestyles and value systems."

Trap 2: Selective legalism

Churches are particularly adept at developing piety systems, where individuals are encouraged to adopt behaviour patterns (usually involving prohibitions) that apparently demonstrate personal holiness and commitment to Christ. Examples of this could be:

● Attendance at a certain number of Christian meetings weekly
● Abstinence from alcohol – not for reasons of choice or personal conscience, but because 'Christians don't drink'
● Codes about dress that go beyond biblical standards of modesty

There is no suggestion in the choice of these illustrations that those who, for example, abstain from alcohol are wrong – they may take these steps because of personal conscience and see it as appropriate behaviour for them as followers of Jesus. But when 'signs of commitment' cease to have a biblical foundation they can quickly degenerate into legalistic 'religious' behaviour, with proud self-justification for those who adhere to the local code and inevitable condemnation for those who don't. Worse still, we can end up feeling we are sufficiently committed to Christ because we satisfy certain culturally generated criteria while actually falling far short of handing our whole life over to him.

OLD TESTAMENT BACKGROUND OF THE BEATITUDES

Ps 1	Blessed is...
Is 57:15	I dwell with him who is contrite and lowly in spirit
Is 61:1	Good news to the poor
Is 61:2	Comfort all who mourn
Ps 37:11	The meek will inherit the land
Is 55:2	Why do you labour for that which does not satisfy?
Ps 18:25 (KJV)	With the merciful you show yourself merciful
Ps 24:3,4	Who shall ascend the hill of the Lord? ... he who has ... a pure heart
Is 51:7	Do not fear the reproach of men or be terrified by their insults.

– Ernest Lucas

SELECTIVE LEGALISM

Some time after World War II, during the reconstruction of Europe, the World Council of Churches wanted to see how its money was being spent in some remote parts of the Balkan peninsula. Accordingly it dispatched John Mackie, who was then the president of the church of Scotland, and two brothers in the cloth of another denomination to take a jeep and travel to some of the villages where the funds were being disbursed.

One afternoon Dr. Mackie and the other two clergymen went to call on the Orthodox priest in a small Greek village. The priest was overjoyed to see them, and was eager to pay his respects. Immediately, he produced a box of Havana cigars, a great treasure in those days, and offered each of his guests a cigar. Dr. Mackie took one, bit the end off, lit it, puffed a few puffs, and said how good it was. The other gentlemen looked horrified and said, "No, thank you, we don't smoke."

Realising he had somehow offended the two who refused, the priest was anxious to make amends. So he excused himself and reappeared in a few minutes with a flagon of his choicest wine. Dr. Mackie took a glassful, sniffed it like a connoisseur, sipped it and praised its quality. Soon he asked for another glass. His companions, however, drew themselves back even more noticeably than before and said, "No, thank you, we don't drink!"

Later, when the three men were in the jeep again, making their way up the rough road out of the village, the two pious clergymen turned upon Dr. Mackie with a vengeance. "Dr. Mackie", they insisted, "do you mean to tell us that you are president of the church of Scotland and an officer of the World Council of Churches and you smoke and drink?"

Dr. Mackie had had all he could take, and his Scottish temper got the better of him. "No, I don't!" he exclaimed, "but somebody had to be a Christian!"

– D.T. Niles, address at Princeton University

PUT IT IN A BOX

"A surprisingly large number of ... Christians have succumbed to a compartmentalized discipleship and a privatized piety. We have compartments in our lives for work, family, recreation, leisure time, vacations, and shopping. And of course, we have one little compartment for church, discipleship, and spiritual life. But in all honesty, the so-called 'secular' compartments tend to dominate our lives, and we Christians are virtually indistinguishable from our non-Christian neighbours. Those who have narrowed God's redemptive activity to that of rescuing our disembodied souls have particularly tended to trivialize what it means to be a disciple and minimize the scope of what God is doing in our world. You see, in the popular understanding of what it means to be a Christian, Christ comes in and transforms our hearts – the spiritual compartment of our lives. ... you can be sure that in the first century the disciples of Jesus weren't doing Roman culture nine to five with church culture on Sundays! They understood that following Christ is a whole life proposition that transforms life directions, values – everything."

– Tom Sine

> "Meekness is essentially a true view of oneself, expressing itself in attitude and conduct with respect to others. ... the one who is truly meek is the one who is truly amazed that God and man can think of him as well as they do and treat him as well as they do."
>
> *– Martin Lloyd Jones*

> "Self-renunciation is the way to world dominion."
>
> *– Rudolph Stier*

> "There is little point in having strong congregations if marriages are falling apart all around us. It doesn't matter if our worship is contemporary if people have no strength or time to nurture their own families. It is of no consequence if the preaching is good, funny or brief if the day-by-day work of the saints is ineffectual. The real battle and place of standing in life and in the heavenly realm is in marriage, family and work."
>
> *– James Thwaites, The Church Beyond the Congregation*

> "Vocation is the response a person makes with his or her total self to the address of God and the calling to partnership. The shaping of vocation ... involves the orchestration of our leisure, our relationships, our work, our private life, our public life, and of the resources we steward, so as to put all at the disposal of God's purposes in the services of God and neighbour."
>
> *– James Fowler*

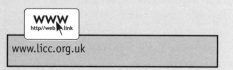

www.licc.org.uk

Trap 3: Sacred-secular dualism

This kind of thinking implies that God works only within the church, at prayer meetings, at worship events, and in spiritual things. This leads us to a:

- Private view of piety
  "I know it's poor ethics, but business is business"
- Narrow view of mission
  "It may be a Christian medical mission, but if there's no preaching I won't support it"
- Restricted view of God at work in history
  "God does not work in the secular world, only in the church"
- Split level vocational thinking – 'spiritual work' and 'secular work'
  "I'm not called to live according to the same standards as a full time Christian leader"
- Irrelevance in teaching
  "No, we've never had a sermon on the workplace, but we had an excellent series on the measurements of the tabernacle"

Pause button

View the various areas of your life. Are they all under the rule and reign of King Jesus? Have some areas dropped to the bottom of your priority list because they're not 'spiritual', even though they're important in God's kingdom?

A challenge:

"Church is not only an activity that happens in certain buildings overseen by pastors. It is in 'all the world' and 'all creation' that we are called to be the body of Christ – to see his church built in our marriages, our businesses, our homes, our work, our gathering together, our entire lives. We must release the powerful name 'church' to define all of life, work and relationships."

– James Thwaites, The Church Beyond the Congregation

ARE YOU ON SSD?

The greatest challenge facing the church.

I had SSD Syndrome for a while. Boy it was tough to cure. And I'm aware that it might flare up again at any time.

In fact, pretty much everyone I know has had it at some time. Pretty much everyone on the Spring Harvest team would tell you they've had it. And it is highly infectious. But on the whole it's easier to detect in others than in yourself.

You can see the effect of SSD in almost every area of life. Here's a teacher commenting on a church with advanced SSD.

"I teach Sunday School 45 minutes a week and they haul me up to the front and the whole church prays for me. I teach school 45 hours a week and no one ever prays for me."

That's SSD: praying for one part of a Christian's life but not another, believing that teaching Sunday school 45 minutes a week is more important to God than teaching school 45 hours a week.

SSD is *sacred-secular divide* – the pervasive belief that some parts of our life aren't really important to God – work, school, leisure – but any to do with prayers, church services, church-based activities are important.

It is because of the sacred-secular divide that over 50% of evangelicals have never heard a sermon on work. It is because of the sacred-secular divide that the vast majority of Christians in every denomination do not feel they get any significant support for their work from the teaching, preaching, prayer, worship, pastoral, group aspects of local church life. No support for how they spend 60–70% of their lives. It is because of the sacred-secular divide that there's hardly a child or adult or youthworker who could give you a Biblical perspective on maths, even though every child in the land spends an hour a day on maths for at least 11 years.

Doesn't Maths teach us something about the rationality of God, about a God for whom truth and accuracy are important? Doesn't Maths give us a window into concepts like infinity and even the Trinity? 1 plus 1 plus 1 equals 3 and The Trinity is unfathomable. But $1 \times 1 \times 1 = 1$ and we can begin to glimpse how three persons might relate to each another and be 1 while still being 3. We teach our kids very young that the 9 to 5 is not important to God.

And it persists. So it was that a senior leader in a large student ministry said:

"I could practically guarantee that you could go into any Christian Union in Britain and not find a single student who could give you a Biblical perspective on the subject they are studying to degree level." That's SSD – not expecting Christians to think Christianly about what they're doing in the world.

Similarly, the national leader of an evangelistic ministry said, "We teach gentle Jesus, meek and mild to teenagers in church. Meanwhile in the world they're studying nuclear physics." That's SSD – setting a lower standard of educational expectation for church teaching than for school, treating adolescents like kids, communicating to them that their mind matters in the world but not in the church.

Sacred-Secular Divide Syndrome leads to people believing that really holy people become missionaries, moderately holy people become ministers and people who are not much use to God get a job. Bah humbug. Sacred-Secular Divide Syndrome leads to people in home groups praying through the prayer letters of overseas missionaries and lifting the names of potential converts to the throne of grace but not knowing the name of the boss of anyone in their home group, never mind praying for them. But doesn't the Bible command us to pray for those in authority?

God is the God of all of life. And Christ claims all of our lives – our life at work and our life in the neighbourhood. If we want to know the joy of whole life Christianity the powerful addictive hallucinogen of SSD must be purged from our bloodstream. If we want to see the West won for Christ, SSD must be expunged from every thought and prayer. After all, most of our interactions with the 92.5% of people who don't know Jesus occur on the secular side of the great divide – the side that we and our communities rarely pray for or consider vital to God.

These are not original ideas but history shows that they are very difficult to live out. SSD is easier to diagnose than to cure. History suggests we will fail. Let's prove history wrong. To the glory of the Lord of all of life.

– Mark Greene, Executive Director of London Institute
for Contemporary Christianity
www.licc.org.uk

King *of the hill*

The Upside Down Kingdom,
Donald Kraybill, Herald Press

THE KING'S ARMS – EXTENDED TO WELCOME

Some argue that the Beatitudes are not primarily a description of Christian character, but a broad invitation to the 'whosoever' in the audience of that day and today to step into the kingdom, the rule of Jesus' love. In this view, the poor in spirit are not blessed *because* they are poor in spirit. They are blessed *despite* their poverty, because of the gracious kiss of Christ upon all who will turn their faces upward to him.

If this were not the case, they argue, one would have to be poor, mournful, persecuted, etc. in order to enter the kingdom and those not fitting these categories would be excluded.

Perhaps there is truth in both approaches to the Beatitudes. Scripture certainly makes it clear that:

- The poor and despised of this world receive a royal welcome from Jesus (Luke 4:16–22; Matt 11:36; Luke 15:1)
- God delights in reversing the normal order of social importance, exalting the humble, humbling the proud, making the first last and the last first, etc (Ex 15; 1 Sam 2, 17; Luke 1).

The King's Arms...

King Jesus invites us to a kingdom lifestyle where everything is different – to put every area of our lives under his authority and reign of love.

He calls us away from merely believing in the right ideas, offering selected parts of our lives to him, or the notion that life is to be lived on two levels – the sacred and the secular.

Every one of us is welcomed by the King of the Hill – he offers the exciting prospect of living under his direction and care. Whoever you are, hear his call and count yourself in.

SPLIT LEVEL VOCATION

In nothing has the church so lost her hold on reality as in her failure to understand and respect the 'secular' vocation. She has allowed work and religion to become separate departments and is astonished to find that, as a result, the secular work of the world is turned to purely selfish and destructive ends and that the greatest part of the world's intelligent workers have become irreligious, or at least uninterested in religion. But is it so astonishing? How can anyone remain interested in a religion which seems to have no concern with nine-tenths of life?"

– *Dorothy Sayers,* Creed or Chaos?

"In the Sermon on the Mount ... the promises attaching, for example, to the so-called 'Beatitudes' must not be regarded as the reward of the spiritual states with which they are respectively connected, nor yet as their result. It is not because a man is poor in spirit that his is the kingdom of heaven, in the sense that one state will grow into the other. The connecting link in each case is Christ himself: because he has opened the kingdom of Heaven to all believers."

– *Alfred Edersheim*

BIBLE PASSAGE

MATTHEW 5:13–48

¹⁴"You are the light of the world. A city on a hill cannot be hidden. ¹⁵Neither do people light a lamp and put it under a bowl. Instead they put it on its stand, and it gives light to everyone in the house. ¹⁶In the same way, let your light shine before men, that they may see your good deeds and praise your Father in heaven.

¹⁷"Do not think that I have come to abolish the Law or the Prophets; I have not come to abolish them but to fulfil them. ¹⁸I tell you the truth, until heaven and earth disappear, not the smallest letter, not the least stroke of a pen, will by any means disappear from the Law until everything is accomplished. ¹⁹Anyone who breaks one of the least of these commandments and teaches others to do the same will be called least in the kingdom of heaven, but whoever practices and teaches these commands will be called great in the kingdom of heaven. ²⁰For I tell you that unless your righteousness surpasses that of the Pharisees and the teachers of the law, you will certainly not enter the kingdom of heaven.

²¹"You have heard that it was said to the people long ago, 'Do not murder, and anyone who murders will be subject to judgment.' ²²But I tell you that anyone who is angry with his brother will be subject to judgment. Again, anyone who says to his brother, 'Raca,' is answerable to the Sanhedrin. But anyone who says, 'You fool!' will be in danger of the fire of hell.

²³"Therefore, if you are offering your gift at the altar and there remember that your brother has something against you, ²⁴leave your gift there in front of the altar. First go and be reconciled to your brother; then come and offer your gift.

²⁵"Settle matters quickly with your adversary who is taking you to court. Do it while you are still with him on the way, or he may hand you over to the judge, and the judge may hand you over to the officer, and you may be thrown into prison. ²⁶I tell you the truth, you will not get out until you have paid the last penny.

²⁷"You have heard that it was said, 'Do not commit adultery.' ²⁸But I tell you that anyone who looks at a woman lustfully has already committed adultery with her in his heart. ²⁹If your right eye causes you to sin, gouge it out and throw it away. It is better for you to lose one part of your body than for your whole body to be thrown into hell. ³⁰And if your right hand causes you to sin, cut it off and throw it away. It is better for you to lose one part of your body than for your whole body to go into hell.

³¹"It has been said, 'Anyone who divorces his wife must give her a certificate of divorce.' ³²But I tell you that anyone who divorces his wife, except for marital unfaithfulness, causes her to become an adulteress, and anyone who marries the divorced woman commits adultery.

³³"Again, you have heard that it was said to the people long ago, 'Do not break your oath, but keep the oaths you have made to the Lord.' ³⁴But I tell you, Do not swear at all: either by heaven, for it is God's throne; ³⁵or by the earth, for it is his footstool; or by Jerusalem, for it is the city of the Great King. ³⁶And do not swear by your head, for you cannot make even one hair white or black. ³⁷Simply let your 'Yes' be 'Yes,' and your 'No,' 'No'; anything beyond this comes from the evil one.

³⁸"You have heard that it was said, 'Eye for eye, and tooth for tooth.' ³⁹But I tell you, Do not resist an evil person. If someone strikes you on the right cheek, turn to him the other also. ⁴⁰And if someone wants to sue you and take your tunic, let him have your cloak as well. ⁴¹If someone forces you to go one mile, go with him two miles. ⁴²Give to the one who asks you, and do not turn away from the one who wants to borrow from you.

⁴³"You have heard that it was said, 'Love your neighbour and hate your enemy.' ⁴⁴But I tell you: Love your enemies and pray for those who persecute you, ⁴⁵that you may be sons of your Father in heaven. He causes his sun to rise on the evil and the good, and sends rain on the righteous and the unrighteous. ⁴⁶If you love those who love you, what reward will you get? Are not even the tax collectors doing that? ⁴⁷And if you greet only your brothers, what are you doing more than others? Do not even pagans do that? ⁴⁸Be perfect, therefore, as your heavenly Father is perfect."

NOTES

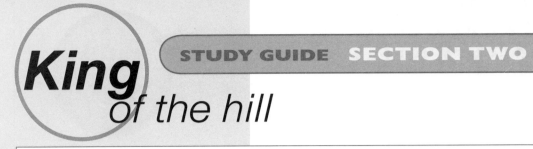

NOTES

THE KING'S CROWN

THE KING'S CROWN – MENU

The Kingdom of God has a different value system – and this session explores some of the reasons why it is so radically different. Holiness and righteousness are key words that we must understand from Jesus' viewpoint.

This session also starts us thinking about parts of God's worldwide church that face persecution and suffering: the King's crown is both a royal diadem and a mocking crown of thorns.

King
of the hill

Challenging Lifestyle, Nicky Gumbel, Kingsway

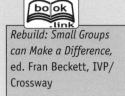

Rebuild: Small Groups can Make a Difference, ed. Fran Beckett, IVP/Crossway

"When the world accepted Christianity, Caesar conquered. The church gave unto God the attributes that belonged exclusively to Caesar. The brief Galilean ministry of humility flickered throughout our ages uncertainly. There is, however, in the Galilean origin of Christianity another suggestion which does not emphasise the ruling Caesar, or the unmoved mover, or the ruthless moralist. A kingdom not of this world it dwells upon the tender elements of the world, which slowly, and in quietness, operate by love."
– Alfred North Whitehead

"The weapons we fight with are not the weapons of the world. On the contrary, they have divine power to demolish strongholds. We demolish arguments and every pretension that sets itself up against the knowledge of God, and we take captive every thought to make it obedient to Christ."
– 2 Cor 10:4–5

THE KING'S CROWN

The King has opened his arms – speaking words that are shocking and revolutionary. He calls us to a different kind of living. No area of our lives will be left untouched by his extended hand; not one of us is excluded from the kingdom invitation.

Today we shall look more closely at some of the details of his royal reign and rule. We will see that although his call is demanding, his offer is also wildly generous. Jesus calls us into the real 'good life' – a superlative, extraordinary level of living. It is the abundant life that Jesus came to give (John 10:10). This is the rich wine of kingdom citizenship, not the tasteless water of mere existence.

And this way of living is far superior to the diluted juice of 'religiosity'. When King Jesus sat down to teach on the hill, there was no shortage of religion – zealous, committed, obsessive religion at that. But throughout his sermon, Jesus repeatedly says: "You have heard… but I tell you… ." He calls us not just to learn about the good life, but to live it.

The King of love

For the crowd that listened to the Sermon, the word king had negative connotations. They had lived under the heel of Herod 'the Great' – a cruel, oppressive despot – and his proud, vain son, Herod Antipas. Herod the Great may have privately owned over half of his kingdom.

The King of the Hill was from a different bloodline. Nazareth, where he was raised, was filled with poor people; most of them had to survive with just one set of clothing. A saying at the time stated: "The daughters of Israel are comely, but their poverty makes them repulsive."

The psalmist describes the ideal king this way:
"For he will deliver the needy who cry out,
the afflicted who have no one to help.
He will take pity on the weak and the needy
and save the needy from death.
He will rescue them from oppression and violence,
for precious is their blood in his sight."
– Psa 72:12–14

THE KING'S CROWN

JESUS THE GOOD KING

Herod the Great was born about the year 73BC and was a son of the desert, well adapted to the political intrigues of ambition, lust for power, and efficiency at warfare. He made a trip to Rome and was confirmed by the senate as 'king of Judea' in the year 40BC. His taxation of the people to support his building activity was extensive, but he virtually rebuilt every city in the land, even constructing entire cities from the ground up. He also built many palaces for himself.

Herod was a paradox. He was one of the most cruel rulers of all history. His reputation has been largely one of infamy. He seemed fiercely loyal to that which he did believe in. He did not hesitate to murder members of his own family when he deemed that they posed a threat to him. He has gone down in history as 'the Great,' yet that epithet can only be applied to him as his personality and accomplishments are compared to others of his family.

Herod Antipas was a son of Herod the Great by his Samaritan wife, Malthace. He was tetrarch of Galilee and Peraea during the whole period of our Lord's life on earth (Luke 23:7). He was a frivolous and vain prince, and was chargeable with many infamous crimes (Mark 8:15; Luke 3:19, 13:31, 32). He beheaded John the Baptist (Matt 14:1–12) at the instigation of Herodias, the wife of his half-brother Herod-Philip, whom he had married.

The Bible teaches that Jesus of Nazareth fulfilled the Old Testament promises of a perfect king and reigns over his people and the universe. The Old Testament hope for the future included a vision of a new king like David called the anointed one, Messiah in Hebrew (2 Sam 7:16). The prophet Isaiah intensified the promises and pointed to the Messiah yet to come (Psa 45; 110). Daniel contains a vision of one to whom was given dominion, glory and kingdom, one whom all peoples, nations and languages would serve. His dominion is everlasting and shall never pass away. His kingdom shall never be destroyed (Dan 7:13–14).

When Jesus Christ was born, his birth was announced in these categories. His earthly ministry then amplified these themes (Matt 4:17; Luke 1:32–33). Similarly, John the Baptist proclaimed the presence of God's kingdom in the coming of Jesus (Matt 3). The theme of Jesus as King, Ruler or Lord dominates the New Testament from beginning to end. We find the culmination of this theme with the Lord seated on a throne, his enemies being made subject to him and a new name given: "On his robe and on his thigh he has this name written: King of kings and Lord of lords." (Rev 19:16)

The present kingship of Christ is his royal rule over his people (Col 1:13, 18). It is a spiritual realm established in the hearts and lives of believers. He administers his kingdom by spiritual means – the Word and the Spirit. Whenever believers follow the lordship of Christ, the Saviour is exercising his ruling or kingly function. From this we understand that his kingship is more concerned with Jesus' reign than with the realm over which this takes place. When we pray "Your kingdom come" as we do in the Lord's prayer (Matt 6:10), we have in mind this present rule of Christ the King.

Christ's kingship is also present today in the natural world. Christ is the one through whom all things came into being (John 1:3) and through whom all things are held together (Col 1:17). He is in control of the natural universe as he demonstrated during his earthly ministry (Mark 4:35–41).

The Bible recognizes Jesus' present kingship and presents the kingship as a spiritual one (John 18:36). The crowd proclaimed Jesus king during his triumphal entry on Palm Sunday (John 12:12–19). We might say the door of heaven opened a bit so that for a brief moment his true kingship appeared to people on earth. He claimed that had the people kept silent on that historic occasion, the stones would have cried out to proclaim him king.

In addition to Christ's present rule, his kingship will become fully evident in the future. We will see and understand this clearly when Jesus returns (Matt 19:28). The future kingdom will be essentially the same as the present rule in the sense that men and women will acknowledge Christ's rule in their hearts. It will differ, however, in that his rule will be perfect and visible (1 Cor 15:24–28). Once manifest, the future kingdom will endure forever. Christ will rule over all things in heaven and on earth. At this time God the Father will exalt Jesus, his son, to the highest place of authority and honour. At the name of Jesus every knee will bow, in heaven and on earth and under the earth, and every tongue will confess that Jesus is Lord to the glory of God the Father (Phil 2:9–11).

Jesus established his kingship through his sacrificial death, as each of the Gospels shows clearly. Pilate recognized more than he knew when he created the sign, King of the Jews, for the charge against Jesus. Jesus' kingship finds its highest exercise as he gives the blessings he secured for his people through his atoning work (Rom 8:32; Eph 1:3–11, 20–22). Jesus will continue to reign as the second person of the Trinity. His God/man personhood will not cease. Jesus Christ, the King, will reign as the God-man and will forever exercise his power for the benefit of the redeemed and for the glory of his kingdom.

– David S. Dockery

King of the hill

Anybody who enters into fellowship with Jesus must undergo a transition of values.

"Recently a pilot was practising high speed manoeuvres in a jet fighter, she turned the controls for what she thought was a steep ascent and flew straight into the ground. She was unaware that she had been flying upside down. This is a parable of human existence in our times – not exactly that everyone is crashing, though there is enough of that – but most of us as individuals, and world society as a whole, live at high speed, and often with no clue to whether we are flying upside down or right side up."

– Dallas Willard

"Purity of heart is to will one thing."

– Søren Kierkegaard

"The Gospel of Christ knows of no religion, but social religion. No holiness, but social holiness."

– John Wesley

"Holiness means being an agent of the incarnation, letting Christ be formed in the church and in the world."

– John Macquarrie

"Like our Lord, who healed the sick and fed the hungry, we must see people as whole people, not as disembodied souls to be prepackaged for heaven."

– Leighton Ford

Christi-Anarchy, Dave Andrews, Lion

Jesus is the king of love, the ultimate people's king who has come out from the splendour of eternal Triune life and has entered our world. His reign, far from being despotic, seeks only to release us from the tyranny of self. It is a revolutionary reign, but one that is riven through with revolutionary love.

This knowledge of God's love gives us the security to allow our thinking to be challenged. It has been said that "anybody who enters into fellowship with Jesus must undergo a transformation of values".

Pause button

Our way of thinking – about God, about life, about everything – can be so fixed that our thinking becomes a mind set. Paul describes some patterns of thinking as "strongholds" and encourages his friends to "take captive every thought to make it obedient to Christ" (2 Cor 10:4,5). Ask God to demolish strongholds in your own thinking today – and pray for courage to allow his royal reign to bring change where it is needed.

Demolishing myths and strongholds

We will see in our journey together today that King Jesus shatters popular myths about success in life:

● Myth number 1:
Success results from putting 'me' first.
In the kingdom, satisfaction comes to those who passionately pursue God's kingdom and his righteousness (Mt 6:33).

● Myth number 2:
Success is about the continual pursuit of personal comfort.
In the kingdom, faithfulness is the ultimate objective, not comfort. This may lead to persecution (Mt 16:24).

● Myth number 3:
Success is to be found in a paradise of personal isolation, where I only have to be concerned about my own needs.
In the kingdom, significance is found in community; in relationships

THE KING'S CROWN

CLASS CONFLICT

First century Palestine had basically two economic classes: upper and lower. In peasant societies rooted in agriculture, 90 per cent or more of the people are usually farmers. Wealth is based on land ownership. So it was in Palestine. A small upper class accounted for 10 per cent or less of the population. These were the landowners, hereditary aristocrats, appointed bureaucrats, chief priests, merchants, government officials, and various official servants who served the needs of the governing class. The rest of the people – like 90 per cent or more – were in the lower class. Living precariously, hand to mouth, they were at the mercy of weather, famine, pestilence, bandit raids and war. There were distinct sub groups in the lower class – at the financial bottom were the outcasts – peasants forced off their land, wandering vagabonds, beggars, lepers. In Galilee, where much of Jesus' ministry took place, the middle class was largely absent. In Galilee, there existed the extremely rich and the miserably poor, the latter being the lot of the majority of the people. The parables and sayings of Jesus assume a two-class system of rich and poor. In spite of many small distinctions, one stark reality dominated the economic landscape: the few lived in luxury while the many lived in harsh poverty.

– Donald Kraybill

⁶Blessed are those who hunger and thirst for righteousness, for they will be filled. ⁷Blessed are the merciful, for they will be shown mercy. ⁸Blessed are the pure in heart, for they will see God. ⁹Blessed are the peacemakers, for they will be called sons of God. ¹⁰Blessed are those who are persecuted because of righteousness, for theirs is the kingdom of heaven. ¹¹"Blessed are you when people insult you, persecute you and falsely say all kinds of evil against you because of me. ¹²Rejoice and be glad, because great is your reward in heaven, for in the same way they persecuted the prophets who were before you."

– Matt 5:6–12

Matthew, JC Ryle, Banner Trust

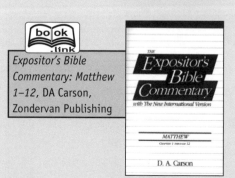

Expositor's Bible Commentary: Matthew 1–12, DA Carson, Zondervan Publishing

that celebrate forgiveness, fidelity and integrity (Col 3:12–17).

● Myth number 4:
Success can be found if I discover the right philosophy or thought system to believe in.
In the kingdom, belief systems are insufficient – whether philosophies, ideas or even doctrines. What counts is our practical response to these beliefs (James 1:22–25).

Real success – kingdom righteousness

But seek first his kingdom and his righteousness, and all these things will be given to you as well (Matt 6:33)

The King's reign leads us from passivity to passion and compassion – hungering and thirsting for righteousness and mercy.

The theme of 'righteousness' runs throughout the Sermon. Subjects of the King:

● may sometimes be persecuted because of righteousness (5:10)
● are called to a righteousness that exceeds that of the scribes and pharisees (5:20)
● are called to do acts of righteousness (6:1)
● are called to seek God's kingdom and his righteousness (6:33)

What is righteousness?

The word 'righteousness' (Greek *dikaiosune*) is difficult to translate exactly, but one common definition for the word is "conformity to a norm". God is righteous, because he conforms willingly to the covenant standards that he established. The New English Bible translates righteousness as 'to see right prevail.' It is certain that the word 'righteousness' has implications not only in our relationship to God, but our relationships with each other, particularly as we have a passion to see right prevail in our world.

There are three types of righteousness in the Bible:

● **Legal righteousness before God.** We are legally described as righteous because of our justification established by Christ in his death and resurrection, and appropriated to us by faith (Rom 9:30–10:4). Christ is our righteousness.
● **Moral righteousness in our ethics and behaviour** – flowing from a righteous heart. The beatitude "Blessed are the pure in heart" is the foundation for all morality. External conformity of behaviour alone is pharisaism – roundly condemned by Jesus,

RIGHTEOUSNESS

Translators have employed 'righteousness' in rendering several biblical words into English: *sedaqah* and *sedeq* in Hebrew; and *dikaiosune* and *euthutes* in Greek. Righteousness in the original languages denotes far more than in English usage; indeed, biblical righteousness is generally at odds with current English usage. We understand righteousness to mean 'uprightness' in the sense of 'adherence or conformity to an established norm.' In biblical usage righteousness is rooted in covenants and relationships. For biblical authors, righteousness is the fulfilment of the terms of a covenant between God and humanity or between humans in the full range of human relationships.

– Holman Bible Dictionary

It is important to acknowledge that, according to Jesus, Christian righteousness has two dimensions – moral and religious. Some speak and behave as if they imagine their major duty as Christians lies in the sphere of religious activity, whether in public (church going) or in private (devotional exercises). Others have reacted so sharply against such an overemphasis on piety that they talk of a 'religionless' Christianity. For them the church has become the secular city, and prayer a loving encounter with their neighbour. But there is no need to choose between piety and morality, religious devotion in church and active service in the world, loving God and loving our neighbour, since Jesus taught that authentic Christian 'righteousness' includes both.

– John Stott, The Sermon on the Mount

Jesus refers to actively seeking the righteousness of the kingdom of God. Godliness involves our actively seeking righteousness in every situation. The Christian has to develop a sense of need. It is only when we are hungry that we cry out to the Lord. "They were hungry … and their lives ebbed away. Then they cried out to the Lord," says Psa 107:5–6. "Come, all you who are thirsty," says Isaiah 55:1. Righteousness is a goal; it is something to aim at. Jesus does not congratulate those who are righteous; he congratulates those who want to be and are thirsty for righteousness. What is it like to be hungry? It tends to distract your attention from anything else you might be doing. A hungry person, whatever else he is doing, tends to be aware that he is hungry! When we 'hunger' for righteousness, it means that whatever else we are doing, this consciousness of God's demand is with us.

It tends to make us push other things aside. A hungry person tends to say to himself, 'Let me get some food, and then I'll do this and that.' A hungry person has a sense of priority. He wants to deal with his hunger first! So with Jesus' hunger for righteousness. It is topmost in our thinking. It is what we are looking for each day. This 'hunger for righteousness' is a desire that God's righteous will should be done in this world, beginning with me! It is a desire to be right with God, to have a good conscience, to be free from the very desire for sin, to be free from gripping self-centredness and defensiveness, to be like Jesus in the way I relate to other people, and to work out God's will for this world in every area where I can make a contribution.

– Michael Eaton, The Way that Leads to Life

There are three angles covered by the word righteousness (*dikaiosune*):

1. Legal – what is sought through the law courts and through appeals to a judge: 'justice'
2. Philosophy – what is fair or equal, what is 'just'
3. Ethical – the behaviour of one who acts 'justly'

So *dikaiosune* and its Hebrew equivalent *sedeq* have something to do with personal piety, but everything to do with living a life which is in accord with the standard of justice set by God. This standard does not simply involve the way we run our personal lives. It involves the way we interact with the society in which we live. Isaiah 58 makes it clear that our lives should be based upon justice – upon values which bring liberation for the oppressed and release the chains of injustice. Micah 6:8 says that what God requires is that we act justly, love his covenant, and walk humbly with God. Righteousness and justice go hand in hand.

With the timely and Holy Spirit-driven rise of social holiness in today's Evangelical churches, the concept of 'justice' is a valid ethical term for *dikaiosune* as a standard which God has set by which we have to live our lives. In the end, we will be judged by this standard: by the standard of justice which God has sown into the web of his creation.

– Peter Phillips

King of the hill

"Mark 14:7 is one of the Bible's most abused texts. It is the saying of Jesus – the poor you will always have with you. People quote it with an air of recognition as if it justified acquiescence in poverty as an insoluble problem instead of spurring action on their behalf. Jesus was quoting Deut 15:11 'There will always be poor people in your land.' And in that same chapter we also read 'there should be no poor among you' (v4). The thrust of the chapter is a call to action, not a surrender to pessimism."

– John Stott, EG Magazine, June 2000

"Just as he who called you is holy, so be holy in all you do; for it is written, 'Be holy, because I am holy.'"

– 1 Peter 1:15-16

Jesus Christ is raging,
   raging in the streets,
where injustice spirals
   and real hope retreats.
Listen, Lord Jesus,
   I am angry too:
in the kingdom's causes
   let me rage with you.

*– by John L. Bell & Graham Maule
copyright © 1988 WGRG, Iona Community,
Glasgow G51 3UU, Scotland.
Reproduced by permission.*

for example in Matthew 23. This purity of heart, an inner commitment to God and his will, is what distinguishes "pagan morality from true Christian holiness" (Michael Eaton). Purity of heart is not merely freedom from lust and evil, but single minded loyalty to God (Psa 24:4, 51:10, 73:1). Teaching about holiness often focuses exclusively on personal sinfulness – living a life of (moral) separation from the corruption that characterizes our amoral culture. We will pick this theme up again later as we consider the teaching of Jesus on anger, murder, divorce and integrity of speech.

- **Social righteousness in our relationships** – causing us to call for right to prevail, in the liberation of the oppressed, in the promotion of human rights, justice, integrity in business, and honour in the home and family (Is 1:21–23, Is 5:7–10, Amos 5:7,10–15). Engaging with and serving our community is positive, biblical and close to God's heart:

- **God has a passion for people**, demonstrated throughout Jesus' ministry and ultimately at the cross. *It's not Christian do-goodism – being nice to hurting people because that's what nice people do.*

- **Holiness is to be expressed in the world** – not away from it. Those who separate themselves physically or emotionally from the needs of the world may find themselves separated from God, who loves his world. *It's not compromise or isolationism, where we misconstrue the moral call of Paul to "come out from them and be separate" (2 Cor 6:17) and then stay as far away from the world and its people as possible.*

- **A concern for the last, the lost and the least has** to be a primary concern for all 'the found'. *It's not an option reserved just for those who feel it's important.*

Pause button

The call to engage with and serve the community is fundamentally a calling to all those who would be followers of the liberating King of the hill. We are all called to be holy (1 Pet 1:15). Holiness without social concern is an unbiblical concept – so Peter's exhortation is to "be holy in all you do."

LET RIGHT PREVAIL

A frail black woman stands slowly to her feet. She is something over 70 years of age.

Facing her from across the room are several white security police officers, one of whom, Mr Van der Broek, has just been tried and found implicated in the murders of both the woman's son and her husband some years before. It was indeed Mr Van der Broek, it has now been established, who had come to the woman's home a number of years back, taken her son, shot him at point-blank range and then burned the young man's body on a fire while he and his officer partied nearby.

Several years later, Mr Van der Broek and his cohorts had returned to take away her husband as well. For many months she heard nothing of his whereabouts.

Then, almost two years after her husband's disappearance, Mr Van der Broek came back to fetch the woman herself. How vividly she remembers that evening, going down to a place beside a river where she was shown her husband, bound and beaten, but still strong in spirit, lying on a pile of wood. The last words she heard from his lips as the officers poured gasoline over his body and set him aflame were, "Father, forgive them."

And now the woman stands in the courtroom and listens to the confessions offered by Mr Van der Broek. A member of South Africa's Truth and Reconciliation Commission turns to her and asks: "So, what do you want? How should justice be done to this man who has so brutally destroyed your family?"

"I want three things," begins the old woman calmly, but confidently. "I want first to be taken to the place where my husband's body was burned so that I can gather up the dust and give his remains a decent burial."

She pauses, then continues. "My husband and son were my only family. I want, secondly, therefore, for Mr Van der Broek to become my son. I would like for him to come twice a month to the ghetto and spend a day with me so that I can pour out on him whatever love I still have remaining within me.

"And finally," she says, "I want a third thing. I would like Mr Van der Broek to know that I offer him my forgiveness because Jesus Christ died to forgive. This was also the wish of my husband. And so, I would kindly ask someone to come to my side and lead me across this courtroom so that I can take Mr Van der Broek in my arms, embrace him and let him know that he is truly forgiven."

As the court assistants come to lead the elderly woman across the room, Mr Van der Broek, overwhelmed by what he has just heard, faints. And as he does, those in the courtroom, friends, family, neighbours – all victims of decades of oppression and injustice – begin to sing, softly, but assuredly, "Amazing grace, how sweet the sound, that saved a wretch like me."

King of the hill

> "The Early Church sought and won her new adherents chiefly among the lower classes in the cities – members of the well to do, educated upper classes only began to enter the church in the second century, and then only very gradually."
>
> – Ernst Troeltsch

> "While he was the Lord of the whole world, he preferred children and ignorant persons to the wise."
>
> – John Calvin

> "The fundamental sympathies of Jesus were with the poor and oppressed."
>
> – Walter Rauschenbusch

> "The uneducated are always a majority with us."
>
> – Tertullian, writing in the 2nd century

> "Everywhere we find the labouring part of mankind the readiest to receive the Gospel."
>
> – John Wesley

> "I was not called to be successful. I was only called to faithful."
>
> – Mother Teresa

Holiness – bad news and good news

1 Pet 1:15 is a direct quotation of Lev 19:2: "Speak to the entire assembly of Israel and say to them: 'Be holy because I, the LORD your God, am holy.' "

The passage then goes on to speak about a holiness that includes:
- family relationships (19:3)
- feeding the poor (19:9)
- doing business with honesty (19:12–14, 35–36)
- looking after the marginalised (19:15)
- environmental responsibility (19:19)
- caring for the elderly (19:32)
- interaction with those of another nationality (19:33)

'Spiritualised' holiness that ignores injustice is *bad news* and is rejected by God: "Yet on the day of your fasting, you do as you please and exploit all your workers." (Isa 58:3)

"Is not this the kind of fasting I have chosen: to loose the chains of injustice and untie the cords of the yoke, to set the oppressed free and break every yoke? Is it not to share your bread with the hungry and to provide the poor wanderer with shelter… ? Then your light will break forth like the dawn, and your healing will quickly appear; then your righteousness will go before you, and the glory of the Lord will be your rear guard." (Isa 58:6–8)

God is angered by this kind of 'holiness':
"I hate, I despise your religious feasts; I cannot stand your assemblies. … Away with the noise of your songs! … But let justice roll on like a river, righteousness like a never failing stream." (Amos 5:21,23–24)

Jesus demonstrated a genuine holiness that is *good news* and is pleasing to the Father (John 17:4):
- Jesus made the preaching of the gospel to the poor a validation of his own ministry. "The spirit of the Lord is upon me, because he has anointed me to preach good news to the poor." (Luke 4:18–21) He plainly said that his practice and conscious intention was to preach the gospel especially to the poor. (Compare Matt 11:1–6)
- Jesus believed the poor were often more ready and able to understand and accept his gospel. (Matt 11:25–26)
- Jesus specifically directed the gospel call to the poor: "Come to

COMPROMISE AND SEPARATISM

The word holy originally referred to 'that which is marked off, withdrawn from ordinary use.' In this early, religious meaning, holiness was the great stranger in the human world.

Some have understood the church's holiness in like manner; the church, they believe, is holy to the extent that it separates itself from the rest of the world. North American fundamentalism of the twentieth century offers the clearest example of this. "By the 1930s," George Marsden writes, "when it became painfully clear that reform from within could not prevent the spread of modernism in major northern denominations, more and more fundamentalists began to make separation from America's major denominations an article of faith … . Some fundamentalists were making separatism into a high principle."

Not only did fundamentalists separate themselves from what they saw as doctrinally wayward denominations, they rigorously and rigidly marked themselves off from the surrounding culture, pointing to Paul's admonition, "What does a believer have in common with an unbeliever? … 'Therefore come out from them and be separate, says the Lord. Touch no unclean thing.'" (2 Cor 6:16–17). Holiness was thus defined as separating oneself from the world, and this was usually defined in negative ways, what one did not do.

The prohibitions were often trivial: a Christian did not smoke, drink, dance, play cards, or go to movies. Though fundamentalists would not have said avoidance of these activities constituted all

there was to holiness, the prevailing ethos implicitly said as much. If non-Christians did these things, Christians did not. It took a good deal of creative proof-texting to make a biblical case against having a glass of wine or watching "It's a Wonderful Life", but the issue had less to do with ethics than being separate.

The church in which I grew up was not especially strict, but I remember sitting in a side room while my third grade classmates learned to dance the hokey-pokey. A note from my parents excused me from this worldly behaviour, and I had to run the record player with Elizabeth, who still spoke with a Norwegian accent, could beat up any boy in the school, and was part of a Pentecostal church.

I don't recall whether I was more embarrassed at not being with my friends or afraid of being with Elizabeth, but I bravely carried my fundamentalist cross. I would never even have considered asking my parents if I could join my buddies on their Saturday afternoon visits to the cinema, that den of wickedness showing Disney movies.

But though holiness, biblically defined, certainly refers to separateness, it knows nothing of separatism, of a withdrawal from the world. A community that makes separatism an end in itself may very well find itself separate not only from the world but from the God who loves this world enough to send the Son to redeem it.

– *adapted from* The Trivialization of God, *Donald McCullough*

King
of the hill

"What a pity that so hard on the heels of Christ come the Christians!"

– Annie Dillard

"Showing mercy to the poor and needy is a touchstone and hallmark of a true conversion to Christ. Without mercy, we are not Christ's, and he shall say to us on the last day (no matter what else we may have achieved), 'I never knew you! Away from me, you evildoers!' (Matt 7:23)."

– Sinclair B Ferguson

"Recreations which bring us into frequent contact with unconverted people are, to say the least, dangerous."

– H.J. Staley, 1872

"The problem with poverty may one day be solved but will the poor or formerly poor still be left without the gospel."

– Howard Snyder

"A church so busily at work correcting the massive injustices of society that it cannot or will not make the effort to win men and women to an allegiance to Jesus Christ will soon become sterile and unable to produce after its kind."

– Ernest Campbell

book link

Holiness in Nineteenth-Century England, David Bebbington, Paternoster

me, all who labour and are heavy laden, and I will give you rest." (Matt 11:28) The universal tendency is to spiritualise these words, but some commentators suggest that they were first addressed to the underclass, who worked long, backbreaking hours . Others believe this to be a call to those who labour under burden of religion.

● Jesus, on several occasions, recommended showing partiality to the poor. (See Matt 19:21; Luke 12:33, 14:12–14)

When we gather up the teaching of Jesus in these few verses and consider his statements

● Blessed are the merciful – verse 7
● Blessed are the peacemakers – verse 9
● You are the salt of the earth – verse 13
● You are the light of the world – verse 14

> We can see that the church is called to be a reconciling people who reach out with mercy (as the good Samaritan showed mercy) and thereby become a people of influence, flavour, light and illumination.

The church – bad news and good news

We, the Christian church, have also to recognize that there are, and have been, times when we do not shine with the brightness that Jesus calls for.

We must face the shame of:

● Silence in the face of totalitarianism – in the German church during Hitler's rise. There were shining exceptions, like Dietrich Bonhoeffer

● Editing out our shameful episodes. For example, writers often celebrate the roots of 'Christian' America. The truth is rather more mixed

● Maintaining a monochrome moral agenda. For example, the issue of abortion is a crucial matter. Thirty million babies have been terminated in the United States under the abortion legislation there. Sometimes, however, the church has been guilty of focusing all its energies on issues such as this and neglecting others, such as homelessness and the care of the environment. Environmentalism therefore became perceived as a 'new age' issue, whereas it should be a primary issue for a people who believe passionately in Father God the Creator, and not in 'mother nature'.

NOT JUST WORDS: THE PERSON OF CHRIST – A PASSION FOR LOVE AND FOR JUSTICE

The political economy in which Jesus grew up was one of total captivity. Palestine was under the complete control of the Roman Empire, abetted as it was by prominent Jewish collaborators. The authorities levied taxes on the population that amounted to 40 per cent of people's income. And their taxes were used to maintain the very army of occupation that the people despised.

When revolts broke out from time to time, as the people tried to break free of the forces that controlled their lives, the Jewish collaborators aided the Roman colonialists in putting down the rebellions. They cooperated with the very powers that oppressed their own people in order to maintain their position, their property and their monopoly of the market. Not surprisingly trade and commerce thrived under the Pax Romana. And the great Jewish Temple in Jerusalem, combining the roles of stock exchange, central bank and government treasury, became the symbol of that prosperity.

However Israel was still essentially an agrarian society. And agriculture was not only the primary industry, but also the premier industry in society. Thus ownership of land was the main source of wealth. Most of the land was owned by a few rich families, who continued to acquire more and more land as the poor families were forced to sell more and more of their land to pay the taxes that were imposed on them. The poor people, who ended up without any land at all, found themselves facing a very bleak future indeed. They were forced to confront a cycle of poverty that entailed not only terrible financial insecurity, but also total fiscal vulnerability to the very system which dispossessed them in the first place.

In this system the poor, the prisoners, the handicapped, the lepers, and other marginalised and disadvantaged people, literally had no one to help them. They were helpless. ...

Jesus grew up with a passionate concern for the welfare of his people, particularly those whom no one else particularly cared for. He was passionately concerned about the plight of the poor, the victims of the imperial system. He was passionately concerned about the predicament of the prisoners and the handicapped, who were excluded from all meaningful participation in society by bars of steel and stigma. He was passionately concerned about the condition of the lepers, not only because of the pain of their ulcers, but also because of the pain of their untouchability. And he was passionately concerned about the situation of ordinary people whose hope had all but been shattered by their soul-destroying circumstances, and who, consequently, felt consigned for ever to long days, and even longer nights of utter despair.

For Jesus, a passionate concern for people meant nothing less than a passionate commitment to them.

He became forgetful of himself, living instead in constant remembrance of those around him, who were themselves forgotten. He desperately wanted them to feel fully alive again, to revel in the joy of being loved, and being able to love, once more. He worked tirelessly to set them free from all that might debilitate them, breaking the bonds of exclusivity, poverty, misery and guilt. He welcomed the outcast, helped the weak, healed the sick, and forgave the sinner, giving them all another chance at a new beginning.

He didn't write anyone off himself, and he encouraged everyone he met not to write one another off either. He challenged everyone to tear up their prejudices, trash their stereotypes, and get their acts together – the in-crowd with the outcast; the strong with the weak; the rich with the poor; the saint with the sinner – to support one another in their common quest for their own humanity.

"The pietist gospel is incomplete if it ignores the social dimensions of righteousness; the social justice gospel is equally incomplete if it ignores the necessity of personal salvation and the importance of personal spirituality and holiness."
— *Rob Warner*

"There is a social movement rooted in worship. It does not consist of activists who happen to have had some background in Christianity. Rather it has right at its centre the person of Jesus, and the activity of worship. This gives it vitality, energy and commitment."
— *Stephen Timmis*

"The left of centre should take note: it is no longer Morris, Keyne and Beveridge who inspire and change the world – it's Leviticus."
— *Will Hutton, writing in The Observer*

"We see organizations born in the church or by Christians – often evangelists or missionaries who look beyond the fabric of the church building to a sense of mission with those excluded or in suffering."
— *Malcolm Hayday, director, Charities Aid Foundation Inspire Fund*

"The indictment of Christianity is just. The complicity of Christian priests, preachers, and missionaries in the cultural destruction and economic exploitation of the primary peoples (of the Americas) is notorious. The certified Christian seems just as likely as anyone to join the military industrial conspiracy to murder Creation!"
— *Wendell Berry, a Christian essayist*

"Instead of seeking the lost sheep – whether black or white or speckled – Protestants sought out those who thought as they thought, and dressed as they dressed, and talked as they talked."
— *David McKenna*

"The failure of the Reformation to meet the religious needs of peasants and other disenfranchised groups is a chapter writ large in history. With all its native religious fervour it remained the religion of the middle class and the nobility."
— *Reinhold Niebuhr*

> But there are many known and unknown evangelical heroes to be thankful for – they are the good news. The call of righteousness drove:

- William Booth to give himself to the "vermin eaten saints with mouldy breath, the unwashed legions with the ways of death" on the streets of London
- Albert Schweitzer, musician, scholar, and medical doctor, to turn his back on comfort and sail for Africa
- Sister Immanuel, at age sixty-four, to ask permission to work among the rubbish pickers in Cairo, Egypt, to educate the children, tell them about Jesus, and help them sort rubbish
- Mother Teresa to establish her home for the dying in Calcutta "so that beggars could die like kings"
- Martin Luther King, the "drum major for righteousness," to lead the American civil rights movement even if it cost him his life
- Countless other unknown people to choose, because they were followers of the King of the Hill, to leave comfort and security to serve others.

Speaking of Jesus, and those that follow him, historian K. S. Latourette writes:

"No life ever lived on this planet has been so influential in the affairs of men … From that brief life and its apparent frustration has flowed a more powerful force for the triumphal waging of man's long battle than any other ever known by the human race … Through it hundreds of millions have been lifted from illiteracy and ignorance, and have been placed upon the road of growing intellectual freedom and of control over their physical environment. It has done more to allay the physical ills of disease and famine than any other impulse known to man. It has emancipated millions from chattel slavery and millions of others from thraldom to vice. It has protected tens

MARTIN LUTHER KING

Here is an excerpt from the sermon King preached at Ebenezer Baptist church on 4 February, 1968, two months before he was assassinated, and which was played at his funeral:

"Every now and then I guess we all think realistically about that day when we will be victimized with what is life's final common denominator – that something we call death. We all think about it. And every now and then I think about my own death, and I think about my own funeral. And I don't think of it in a morbid sense. Every now and then I ask myself, 'What is it that I would want said?' And I leave the word to you this morning.

If any of you are around when I have to meet my day, I don't want a long funeral. And if you get somebody to deliver the eulogy, tell them not to talk too long. Every now and then I wonder what I want them to say. Tell them not to mention that I have a Nobel Peace Prize, that isn't important. Tell them not to mention that I have three or four hundred other awards, that's not important. Tell them not to mention where I went to school.

I'd like somebody to mention that day that Martin Luther King tried to give his life serving others. I'd like for somebody to say that day that Martin Luther King tried to love somebody. I want you to say that day that I tried to be right on the war question. I want you to be able to say that day that I did try to feed the hungry. And I want you to be able to say that day that I did try, in my life, to clothe those who were naked. I want you to say on that day that I did try, in my life, to visit those who were in prison. I want you to say that I tried to love and serve humanity. Yes, if you want to say that I was a drum major, say that I was a drum major for justice. Say that I was a drum major for peace, I was a drum major for righteousness.

And all of the other shallow things will not matter. I won't have any money to leave behind. I won't have the fine and luxurious things of life to leave behind. I just want to leave a committed life behind.

And that's all I want to say ... if I can help somebody as I pass along, if I can cheer somebody with a word or song, if I can show somebody he's travelling wrong then my living will not be in vain. If I can do my duty as a Christian ought, if I can bring salvation to a world over wrought, if I can spread the message as the Master taught, then my living will not be in vain."

The people of God are tempted to absorb the values around them. It's easy to temper the gospel by making it pleasant to the majority. And before we know it, we borrow the ideology, the logic, and the bureaucratic structures of our neighbours. We might put a little religious Teflon on top, but underneath the values and procedures clash with the way of Jesus. The organizational structures of our churches must be functional and relevant to our cultural context without being determined by it. The moment the church capitulates to the world, the light is dimmed, the salt turns tasteless, and the leaven leaves. Participation in Christian community undergirds our spiritual and emotional well being. Following the beat of a different drummer requires a community of others to provide needed support and affirmation.

– Donald Kraybill

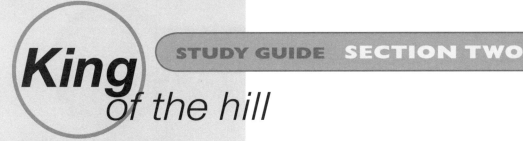

King
of the hill

of millions from exploitation by their fellows. It has been the most fruitful source of movements to lessen the horrors of war and to put the relations of men and nations on the basis of justice and peace."

Are we good news?

Let's reflect on some of the key points we have seen so far today:

- We must have a balance of word and works together
- Our concern must be with the central truth of the gospel message: reconciliation between God and man through the blood of Jesus Christ. This is not narrow thinking but a faithfulness to the priority that Jesus himself set when he spoke of preaching good news to the poor. (Luke 4:18; Matt 11:5)
- We must not overreact against a past preoccupation with saving souls and abandon the proclamation of the good news: nothing that we can do for the poor is better than holistic evangelism, where practical support runs alongside preaching the gospel
- The gospel changes people. Are we more concerned with poverty than the poor? Are we more committed to programmes than to people? Is our first interest to solve the social problem or meet a personal need?
- Beware of moralism – works without the breath and life of God
- Beware of separatism – 'holiness' without the arena of community

Bob Holman, professor of Social Administration at Bath University, has chosen to live on Europe's largest public housing estate, Easterhouse in Glasgow. He has co-written a remarkable book, titled *Faith in the Poor*, with seven residents of the infamous estate; his work is an attempt to give a voice to those who would often be marginalised.

"Jesus was astonishingly radical in that he called and gave responsibility to those who socially and materially were in the bottom percentage of the time," Holman says.

Pause button
What are you? Are you good news or bad news in your community? If a survey was run in your area, would others in the community consider your church to be good news or bad news?

THE KING'S CROWN

THE JUBILEE 2000 CAMPAIGN

People's experience in churches and the changes brought about in their lives when they start to follow Jesus are becoming a major influence on society. That may seem naive at a time when newspapers report gleefully that attendance at church has plummeted. But whatever the statistics, it is clear that church commitment and engagement in social action, as well as financial giving, are sharply rising.

Take the remarkable impact of the Jubilee 2000 campaign. From the black churches in London to parish churches in some of the most affluent parts of the country, something pretty extraordinary has occurred. Of course, it has not been an exclusively Christian campaign – it has won very wide support, and that has been one of its glories. But 80 per cent of those who have participated in the human chains, and sent the 'drop the debt' postcards, come from the churches. There has not been anything like it since the campaign against the slave trade.

Will Hutton reflected in the Observer: "At the end of an increasingly secular century, it has been the biblical proof and moral imagination of religion that have torched the principles of hitherto unassailable citadels of international finance – and opened the way to a radicalism about capitalism whose ramifications are not yet fully understood. There is the moral basis for a new social settlement. The left of centre should take note: it is no longer Morris, Keyne and Beveridge who inspire and change the world – it's Leviticus."

EMPOWERMENT SPEAKS LOUDER THAN ACTIONS

However, we must serve and empower people rather than 'do things' to them. Some 'social action projects' have the effect of removing the dignity of those that they seek to reach and serve. When we take action without taking time to listen, or make judgments about solutions without ever consulting with and learning from those with the problems, we disenfranchise and dehumanize the poor.

This kind of action will mean that:
- Our efforts fail, because they are not as focused as they should be
- Our efforts then become charitable tokenism rather than strategic action
- We then serve ourselves, feeding a personal 'feel-good' factor rather than doing much real good
- The poor are stereotyped by our ignorance
- We view the problems through the eyes of those "experts" who are themselves outsiders to the problems
- We continue to contribute to the sense of powerlessness felt by the poor by perpetuating their powerlessness

"One phase of the history of denominationalism reveals itself as the story of the religiously neglected poor, who fashion a new type of Christianity which corresponds to their distinctive needs, who rise in economic scale under the influence of religious discipline, and who in the midst of a freshly acquired social respectability, neglect the new poor succeeding them on the lower plane. This pattern recurs with remarkable regularity in the history of Christianity."

– H. Richard Niebuhr, Social Sources of Denominationalism, 1929

¹⁰**Blessed are those who are persecuted because of righteousness, for theirs is the kingdom of heaven.** ¹¹**"Blessed are you when people insult you, persecute you and falsely say all kinds of evil against you because of me.** ¹²**Rejoice and be glad, because great is your reward in heaven, for in the same way they persecuted the prophets who were before you."**

– Matt 5:10–12

book.link

Jesus Freaks, dc Talk and the Voice of the Martyrs, Eagle Publishing

PERSECUTED FOR RIGHTEOUSNESS

It is not only the materially poor that find themselves the victims of oppression. Those who hunger and thirst for the righteousness of Jesus are certainly to expect persecution.

The Early Church was slandered mercilessly with charges that included:

- **Incest** – because Christians called one another 'brother' and 'sister'
- **Murdering babies and cannibalism** – because Christians spoke of eating Christ's body and drinking his blood in their worship meetings
- **Atheism** – because Christians showed neither respect nor fear for the Roman pantheon of gods
- **Disloyalty to the emperor** – because Christians refused to offer worship to Caesar or make the confession 'Caesar is Lord'
- **Irreligion** – because the Christians had neither altars, temples nor priests
- **Sexual perversions and orgies** – because the Christians met at night
- **No appreciation of social status** – because the Christians welcomed all as equals. Tatian spelled out the radical equality so despised by the class-conscious snobs of the empire: "We do not make any distinctions in rank and outward appearance, or wealth and education, or age and sex."

> **For us, this may mean that we suffer minor rejection, or some experience of being ostracized because of our faith.**

We should note that persecution:
- Should be because of righteousness (v10) – not because of obnoxiousness
- Must be considered in the context of an eternal perspective (v10)
- Is a privilege because we are enabled to identify with Jesus (v11)
- Is therefore a cause for celebration – we are called to be glad. One translation says, "Leap for joy" (v12).

"MORE LOVE TO THEE"
Pastor Kim and his congregation, North Korea, 1950s

For years, Pastor Kim and 27 of his flock of Korean saints had lived in hand-dug tunnels beneath the earth. Then, as the communists were building a road, they discovered the Christians living underground.

The officials brought them out before a crowd of 30,000 in the village of Gok San for a public trial and execution. They were told, "Deny Christ, or you will die." But they refused.

At this point the head communist officer ordered four children from the group seized and had them prepared for hanging. With ropes tied around their small necks, the officer again commanded the parents to deny Christ.

Not one of the believers would deny their faith. They told the children, "We will soon see you in heaven." The children died quietly.

The officer then called for a steamroller to be brought in. He forced the Christians to lie on the ground in its path. As its engine revved, they were given one last chance to recant their faith in Jesus. Again they refused.

As the steamroller began to inch forward, the Christians began to sing a song they had often sung together. As their bones and bodies were crushed under the pressure of the massive rollers, their lips uttered the words:

More to love thee, O Christ, more to love thee
Thee alone I seek, more love to thee
Let sorrow do its work, more love to thee
Then shall my latest breath whisper thy praise
This be the parting cry my heart shall raise;
More love, O Christ, to thee.

The execution was reported in the North Korean press as an act of suppressing superstition.

– Jesus Freaks, *Eagle Publishing, pg 124*

PAKISTAN
In Pakistan today, any form of blasphemy, by imputation or insinuation, against the prophet Mohammed carries with it a mandatory sentence of death. The law has been used as a foil to intimidate and falsely accuse Christians who try to live out their faith.

Catherine Shaheen is a living symbol of the Persecuted Church.

Catherine - a Christian in Pakistan - was a brilliant head teacher with a promising career. She was forced to go into hiding for four years after jealous colleagues orchestrated a false blasphemy charge against her.

A judicial panel cleared her of all charges but outraged Muslim extremists continued to terrorise her. When Catherine's sisters joined her in hiding, police detained her father and brother. Both were beaten while in custody in an attempt to find their hiding place. Catherine's brother was held for 15 months but sadly her father died two months after the assault.

When fear of assassination increased, a Jubilee team was sent to rescue Catherine and she and her sister now live in safety in another country.

King of the hill

"Christian faithfulness is not necessarily measured by where one lives, although in some cases it may be. The basic issue is Christian responsibility for the poor. If Christians move from a certain area, they must ask themselves what this move means for their responsibility towards the poor. What are their motives for moving? Where can they best build the church? Are they leaving the poor behind? If so, whose responsibility are the poor? Does the move represent greater or less obedience to the gospel? Facing such hard questions in the light of the Scriptures may be the only way to break the pattern of leaving the poor spiritually disinherited."
– Howard A. Snyder

"The problem is not that Christians prosper, it is that in prospering they tend to turn their back on the poor and adopt the social attitudes of their newly acquired status. Consciousness of the gospels special call to the poor is either forgotten or spiritualised."
– Howard A. Snyder

book link

Hidden Sorrow, Lasting Joy: The Forgotten Women of the Persecuted church, Anneke Companjen, Hodder & Stoughton

Paying a higher price – the suffering church

For many of our brothers and sisters around the world, persecution means far more than enduring an occasional cutting comment.

It is said that there are more Christian martyrs today than there were in AD100 – in the days of the Roman Empire. According to World Christian Encyclopedia, there were close to 164,000 Christians martyred around the world in 1999. An estimated 165,000 were martyred in 2000.

In a sense, Jesus is in jail: "For I was hungry …" Matt 25:35–46

Here are some practical steps we can take to support our brothers and sisters in the suffering church:

- **Stay informed.** We need to know who is persecuted for their faith in Christ and where. Remember, Scripture tells us to remember the prisoners as if we were imprisoned with them (Heb 13:3).
- **Pray.** Many Christians who have undergone persecution recount that the knowledge that others were praying for them was vital to them.
- **Encourage.** There are many instances where letters and cards from abroad have greatly encouraged persecuted Christians. A few words from a child have shed light in darkness. Letters and cards show that, though isolated, a person is not forgotten. It reminds those who suffer that other members of Christ's body care about their situation. Help is available to direct writers to those in need of encouragement, as well as direction about what you can say in your letters without causing problems for the persons to whom you write.
- **Participate.** One way to become involved with the persecuted church is to become an 'advocate' for suffering Christians around the world. An advocate, according to Webster's Dictionary, is someone who 'pleads the cause of another … defends, vindicates, or espouses a case by argument; is friendly to an upholder; a defender'.
- **Campaign.** In some cases, political pressure can make a big difference. Writing letters to ambassadors, members of parliament, congressman, presidents and others in authority – these are all ways in which we can lighten the burden of those who are persecuted for their faith.

CHINA

Bob and Heidi Fu were leaders in the student movement in China in the late '80s and were along the radicals who protested in Tiananmen Square. Bob graduated in International Politics and Heidi studied philosophy.

They were clearly destined for influential positions, but in the aftermath of the Tiananmen massacre, disillusioned with the system, they came to a personal faith. Working with the underground church, they set up an effective training centre and quickly became key leaders in the church.

In 1997, they were arrested and jailed for two months. Following their release, they were given two months to vacate their apartment. An insider warned them that they were in great danger if they did not leave.

So Bob and Heidi escaped China and went into hiding in Hong Kong.

However, they were still not safe. They faced being sent to prison again when Hong Kong was handed back to China in just 21 days. Jubilee's Danny Smith felt compelled to go help them escape once again.

After an agonising struggle, with 48 hours to spare, Bob and Heidi managed to leave Hong Kong, safe and well. Throughout they had told us 'We rely on God alone. We're in his hands.'

The atheist Communist State still does not allow Christians to practice their faith. Millions of Christians are forced into illegal underground churches and are often imprisoned and tortured if found. Hundreds of churches are still being blow-up or closed down every year.

A SIMPLE THING

I'll tell you a little story which I told in Damascus. I was kept in total and complete isolation for four years. I saw no one and spoke to no one apart from a cursory word with my guards when they brought me food. And one day, out of the blue, a guard came into my room with a postcard; it was a postcard of the stained-glass window from Bedford showing John Bunyan in jail, and I looked at that card and I thought, My word, Bunyan, you're a lucky fellow, you've got a window out of which you can look and see the sky and here I am in a dark room; you've got pen and ink and you can write and I've got nothing; and you've got your own clothes and a table and a chair; and I turned the card over and there was a message from someone whom I didn't know simply saying, We remember, we shall not forget, we shall continue to pray for you and to work for all people who are detained around the world. I can tell you, that thought sent me back to the marvellous work of agencies like Amnesty International and their letter-writing campaigns. I would say to you all, never despise those simple actions. Something, somewhere, will get through to the people you are concerned about, as it got through to me and to my fellow hostages eventually.

– Terry Waite, Taken on Trust, Hodder and Stoughton

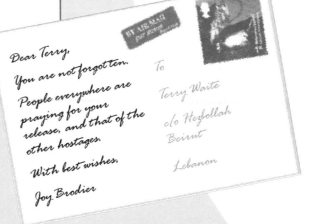

Dear Terry,
You are not forgotten. People everywhere are praying for your release, and that of the other hostages.
With best wishes,
Joy Brodier

To
Terry Waite
c/o Hezbollah
Beirut
Lebanon

"I was hungry and you gave me a press release."

Righteousness is a demanding call that will disrupt and bring inconvenience to our lives. No longer preoccupied with our own personal prosperity, we join the King of the hill in laying down our lives for the persecuted and the poor. We will continue to explore this tomorrow.

"If you have the hearts of Christians and of men, let them yearn towards your poor, ignorant, ungodly neighbours. Alas, there is but a step between them and death and hell. Have you hearts of rock, that you cannot pity men in such a case as this? If you believe not the Word of God, and the dangers of sinners, why are you Christians yourselves? If you do believe it, why do you not bestir yourselves to the helping of others? Do you not care who is damned, as long as you are saved?"

– *Richard Baxter*

Pause button
You did it for me

What are the situations – small and large – where you encounter the hungry, the thirsty, the stranger, those needing material or personal support? Ask God to prompt you about how to respond: "whatever you did for the least of these brothers of mine, you did for me."

"Speak up for those who cannot speak for themselves, for the rights of all who are destitute. Speak up and judge fairly; defend the rights of the poor and needy."

– *Prov 31:8–9*

YES, I BELIEVE IN GOD

She was 17 years old. He stood glaring at her, his weapon before her face.

"Do you believe in God?"

She paused. It was a life or death question. "Yes. I believe in God."

"Why?" her executioner asked. But he never gave her the chance to respond.

The teenage girl lay dead at his feet.

> *This scene could have happened in the Roman coliseum. It could have happened in the Middle Ages. And it could have happened in any number of countries around the world today. People are being imprisoned, tortured, and killed every day because they refuse to deny the name of Jesus.*
>
> *This particular story, though, did not happen in ancient times, nor in Vietnam, Pakistan or Romania. It happened at Columbine High School in Littleton, Colorado, on April 20, 1999.*
>
> *Do you believe in Jesus?*
>
> – Jesus Freaks, *Eagle Publishing*

BIBLE PASSAGE

MATTHEW
6:1–34

¹"Be careful not to do your 'acts of righteousness' before men, to be seen by them. If you do, you will have no reward from your Father in heaven.

²"So when you give to the needy, do not announce it with trumpets, as the hypocrites do in the synagogues and on the streets, to be honoured by men. I tell you the truth, they have received their reward in full. ³But when you give to the needy, do not let your left hand know what your right hand is doing, ⁴so that your giving may be in secret. Then your Father, who sees what is done in secret, will reward you.

⁵"And when you pray, do not be like the hypocrites, for they love to pray standing in the synagogues and on the street corners to be seen by men. I tell you the truth, they have received their reward in full. ⁶But when you pray, go into your room, close the door and pray to your Father, who is unseen. Then your Father, who sees what is done in secret, will reward you. ⁷And when you pray, do not keep on babbling like pagans, for they think they will be heard because of their many words. ⁸Do not be like them, for your Father knows what you need before you ask him.

⁹"This, then, is how you should pray:

"   'Our Father in heaven,
      hallowed be your name,
¹⁰   your kingdom come,
      your will be done on earth as it is in heaven.
¹¹   Give us today our daily bread.
¹²   Forgive us our debts, as we also have
      forgiven our debtors.
¹³   And lead us not into temptation,
      but deliver us from the evil one.'

¹⁴For if you forgive men when they sin against you, your heavenly Father will also forgive you. ¹⁵But if you do not forgive men their sins, your Father will not forgive your sins.

¹⁶"When you fast, do not look sombre as the hypocrites do, for they disfigure their faces to show men they are fasting. I tell you the truth, they have received their reward in full. ¹⁷But when you fast, put oil on your head and wash your face, ¹⁸so that it will not be obvious to men that you are fasting, but only to your Father, who is unseen; and your Father, who sees what is done in secret, will reward you.

¹⁹"Do not store up for yourselves treasures on earth, where moth and rust destroy, and where thieves break in and steal. ²⁰But store up for yourselves treasures in heaven, where moth and rust do not destroy, and where thieves do not break in and steal. ²¹For where your treasure is, there your heart will be also.

²²"The eye is the lamp of the body. If your eyes are good, your whole body will be full of light. ²³But if your eyes are bad, your whole body will be full of darkness. If then the light within you is darkness, how great is that darkness!

²⁴"No one can serve two masters. Either he will hate the one and love the other, or he will be devoted to the one and despise the other. You cannot serve both God and Money.

²⁵"Therefore I tell you, do not worry about your life, what you will eat or drink; or about your body, what you will wear. Is not life more important than food, and the body more important than clothes? ²⁶Look at the birds of the air; they do not sow or reap or store away in barns, and yet your heavenly Father feeds them. Are you not much more valuable than they? ²⁷Who of you by worrying can add a single hour to his life?

²⁸"And why do you worry about clothes? See how the lilies of the field grow. They do not labour or spin. ²⁹Yet I tell you that not even Solomon in all his splendour was dressed like one of these. ³⁰If that is how God clothes the grass of the field, which is here today and tomorrow is thrown into the fire, will he not much more clothe you, O you of little faith? ³¹So do not worry, saying, 'What shall we eat?' or 'What shall we drink?' or 'What shall we wear?' ³²For the pagans run after all these things, and your heavenly Father knows that you need them. ³³But seek first his kingdom and his righteousness, and all these things will be given to you as well. ³⁴Therefore do not worry about tomorrow, for tomorrow will worry about itself. Each day has enough trouble of its own.

7:1–6

¹"Do not judge, or you too will be judged. ²For in the same way you judge others, you will be judged, and with the measure you use, it will be measured to you.

³"Why do you look at the speck of sawdust in your brother's eye and pay no attention to the plank in your own eye? ⁴How can you say to your brother, 'Let me take the speck out of your eye,' when all the time there is a plank in your own eye? ⁵You hypocrite, first take the plank out of your own eye, and then you will see clearly to remove the speck from your brother's eye.

⁶"Do not give dogs what is sacred; do not throw your pearls to pigs. If you do, they may trample them under their feet, and then turn and tear you to pieces."

THE KING'S COMMUNITY

NOTES

NOTES

THE KING'S COMMUNITY – MENU

God has called us to be something corporately, as well as individually. We call it church. This session looks at God's intention and how far we have drifted from it. What are the practical consequences of that little phrase, "salt and light"?

Working through some of the most challenging words of the Great Sermon, we think through some of the hallmarks that will be seen in those who turn talk into action as part of the King's Community.

THE KING'S COMMUNITY

HALLMARKS OF THE KING'S COMMUNITY

King
of the hill

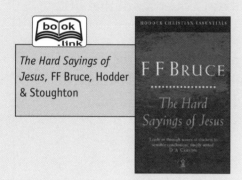

book.link

God was in Christ, Donald Baillie, Charles Scribners and Sons

book.link

The Hard Sayings of Jesus, FF Bruce, Hodder & Stoughton

When I entrust myself to God – I lose my disobedient egocentricity; but I gain the self I was created to be. I become a person-in-community, a person in fellowship with God and others. Emil Brunner aptly describes this change:

"That is faith: a change of hands, a revolution, an overthrow of government. A lord of self becomes one who obeys – solitariness is now also past. The imperious, reserved 'I' is broken open; into my world, in which I was alone – into the solitariness of the 'Thou-less' I, God has stepped in as Thou. He who believes is never solitary. Faith is the radical overcoming of the I-solitariness. The monologue of existence – even that existence in which many things have been talked about with many people – has now become the dialogue of existence: now there is unconditional fellowship."

THE KING'S COMMUNITY

Called to Community

The King has established a community to live out the truth, a demonstration, a model for planet earth to see life as God intended it to be lived. The message of the kingdom is more than a theologically correct idea to be preached – it is a lifestyle to be lived, expressed as a community where:

- God is at the centre of our individual and communal lives
- Life is celebrated with the poor and the outcasts
- The stranger is welcomed
- God is served with true righteousness
- The values of God's new order are fleshed out
- Relationships are profoundly valuable – not disposable items
- Faithfulness is esteemed
- Reconciliation is practised on a daily basis

We call it church

The church is quite unlike any other collective group on planet earth. It is far more than:

- a morally upright group of people who get together for fellowship because they believe the same things
- a lecture hall which provides an environment for the development of biblical understanding
- a theatre where the faithful gather to see the drama of the sacrament acted out before them
- a corporation with a streamlined mission statement and a professional team of executives who do the work of the ministry
- a social club that people join in order to get their needs met.

Among many other things the church is:

- The royal household ("God's household," Eph 2:19)
- The primary royal ambassador and agent of the kingdom with the ministry of reconciliation (Eph 1:10; Col 1:20)
- The royal herald and revelation of the wisdom of God (Eph 3:10)
- The flock of God (1 Peter 5:2)
- A living temple of the Holy Spirit (Eph 2:21–22)
- The object of Christ's passion (Eph 5:25)
- A body that straddles heaven and earth (Eph 1:3, 2:6, 3:10)
- The object of God's architectural master plan (Matt 16:18)
- The bride of Christ (Rev 21:9)
- The body of Christ (1 Cor 12:27)

A COMMUNITY

Donald Baillie provides a memorable image of a tale of God calling his human children to form a great circle for the playing of his game:

In that circle we ought all to be standing, linked together with lovingly joined hands, facing towards the light in the centre, which is God ("the love that moves the sun and the other stars"); seeing our fellow creatures all round the circle in the light of that central love, which shines on them and beautifies their faces; and joining with them in the dance of God's great game, the rhythm of love universal. But instead of that, we have, each one, turned our backs upon God and the circle of our fellows, and faced the other way, so that we can see neither the light at the centre nor the faces on the circumference. And indeed in that position it is difficult even to join hands with our fellows! Therefore instead of playing God's game we play, each one, our own selfish little game... . Each one of us wishes to be the centre, and there is blind confusion, and not even any true knowledge of God or of our neighbours. That is what is wrong...

THE STRANGER IS WELCOMED

In his novel *Walking Across Egypt*, Clyde Edgerton tells about Mattie Rigsbee, a woman in her late 70's who lives alone in simplicity and wisdom. At one point in the story, Mattie takes in a young scalawag, Wesley, who has escaped from a detention centre. One Saturday night, she asks him if he has ever been to church. He says no; he has been by one, seen one on television, but never actually been in one. Edgerton then describes what went on in Mattie's mind:

"Mattie saw before her a dry, dying plant which needed water up through the roots – a pale boy with rotten teeth who needed the cool nourishing water of hymns sung to God, of kind people speaking to him, asking him how things were going, the cool water of clean people, clean children, old people being held by the arm and helped up a flight of stairs, old people who looked with thanks up into the eyes of their helpers, of young and old people sitting together for one purpose: to worship their Maker, to worship Jesus, to do all that together and to care for each other and to read and sing and talk together about God and Jesus and the Bible. That would bring colour to his cheeks, a robustness to his bearing. That would do it. He seemed smart enough. And, since he hadn't been to church, then he was lost; this could be his first stop on the road to salvation."

The Church in the Power of the Spirit, Jurgen Moltmann, SCM Press

"A new community has been formed by the gracious invitation of God's holiness."

– Donald McCullough

"For God was pleased to have all his fullness dwell in him, [20]and through him to reconcile to himself all things, whether things on earth or things in heaven, by making peace through his blood, shed on the cross."

– Col 1:19–20

"The political novelty which God brings into the world is a community of those who serve instead of ruling, who suffer instead of inflicting suffering, whose fellowship crosses social lines instead of reinforcing them. This new Christian community is not only a vehicle of the gospel or the fruit of the gospel; it is the good news."

– John Howard Yoder

"The divine story will impact only to the extent to which the saints know how to live it in a postmodern age. In this stage of the story we need to empower the saints for much more than church life and its programmes. We need to equip them to be the divine and eternal story in all of life and work."

– James Thwaites

"We are the bibles that the world are reading."

– Billy Graham

Postmodern culture is preoccupied with individualism. There is a type of Christianity that so emphasises the truth that Jesus is my 'personal' saviour that I lose sight of the vision of kingdom community so powerfully expressed in the images above.

When we lose sight of the collective nature of the kingdom, we tend to treat the church as an organisation that exists simply to nurture our own personal relationship with God, rather than as an agent of the kingdom of God, and an expression of the radical kind of relationships that kingdom living demands.

Christians who are obsessively diligent about personal devotions and private piety, but who are difficult and offensive in their inter-personal relationships, have lost the sense of priority that God places upon working out our salvation life together.

A community of the Cross

The church is also the community that has come about because of the work of atonement and reconciliation that was wrought at the Cross. Christ therefore is to be the centre of this new kingdom community – and the Father in heaven will be glorified as the church lives out the kingdom life.

In the course of the Sermon on the Mount, Jesus uses a number of word-pictures and metaphors to describe the essential nature of his kingdom community. These pictures have much to say to us about our identity, our priorities, and the nature of our relationships together. Initially three pictures emerge: salt, light and a city set on a hill.

'Don't look at the church, look at Jesus' is a statement we Christians often make, because we are embarrassed by the obvious weaknesses of the church. But God has designed the church to be a prophetic community to the world – a body that does more than just preach about the truth – rather a community that is the truth: one that embodies and demonstrates what life under the reign of King Jesus is actually like in a very visible manner – like a city on a hill, or a beacon that flares in the darkness. Just as salt has a sharp, distinctive flavour, so this community is to 'season' the bland world into which she has been placed. A church that aspires to anything less is literally useless – "no longer good for anything" (Matt 5:13).

THE KING'S COMMUNITY

WHAT IS THE CHURCH FOR?

Worship – Lifestyle – Fellowship – Witness

1. Worshipping God
2. Living the kingdom in the world – incarnation, social holiness, justice, healing, challenge, counter-culture,
3. Being the body of Christ to one another – fellowship, discipleship, healing, teaching
4. Proclaiming the Word – ambassadors, witnesses in word and deed, talking the talk and walking the walk

– Peter Phillips

UNKNOWN HEROES:
THE EASTERHOUSE SALVATION ARMY

Church attendance is notoriously low on council estates. The Easterhouse Corps of the Salvation Army was under the leadership of Captain Eric and Mrs Anne Buchanan. They are now retired, following the captain suffering a stroke.

The Buchanans were not brought up as Salvationists and did not enter its ministry until middle age. Consequently, they were not steeped in tradition. For most of their time in Easterhouse, they lived in rooms above two small halls, one for worship, one for social activities. In run down condition and with the windows covered with wire and boards, the building was sometimes known as 'the fortress'.

Captain Buchanan was forceful, outspoken and devoted to Easterhouse. On the one occasion, the hall was packed for the Christmas carol service. Mrs Buchanan was in the small hall dressing the children for the nativity play. The captain was leading with his usual gusto when he spotted a man entering the back door. He was obviously in need of help and the captain just walked out to assist him. The meeting came to a puzzled silence for several minutes before someone else rose to organize community singing. His concern for that man was such that he forgot everything else.

Captain Buchanan considered the Christian gospel to be about material help and personal support to the needy. His outgoing manner and machine-gun-like questions did offend some people, yet others responded. Interestingly, a number of drug-abusers invited him in and trusted him. His concern for material needs did not mean, however, that he disregarded the call to people to make a personal relationship with God. The Sunday evening meeting

was evangelical in nature and often ended with an invitation to kneel at the mercy seat. On such occasions, the captain would signal to a uniformed member to counsel the kneeling person.

Carol first approached the Salvation Army when her brother moved to Easterhouse. She wrote as follows:

"I went along to the Salvation Army to get some second-hand furniture for him. It was there I met Captain Buchanan. I could hardly believe him. In his old, baggy pullover, if it wasn't for his Salvation Army cap you would have thought he had come in looking for somewhere to stay. He was always rushing around for people. He was a bit like myself, he thought for others not for himself.

"I started going to the services on a Sunday. The Social Work Department was getting really heavy with me and I was looking for someone to turn to apart from my dad. I was so mixed up and I wanted to test myself, 'Do I believe or not believe?' And if I did believe I wanted to know why all these things were happening to me. I got my daughter christened at the *Sally*. I started helping the captain at a Tuesday lunch club which he started for men, mostly alcoholics. I enjoyed that. When I saw the look on some of the guys' faces when I gave them mince and tatties, it made me realize how lucky I was... . I enjoyed the services at the Sally and looked forward to them. I met friends there. ... people who never held ill feelings against you. They always wanted to help, they gave me time and explained things. The Social Work Department had taken away all my confidence. At times I could not talk. I would just break down. I started to believe in God for selfish reasons at first. He was the only one who I could talk to and did not say bad things to me. God listened and gave me strength."

King of the hill

Matthew 5

¹³"You are the salt of the earth. But if the salt loses its saltiness, how can it be made salty again? It is no longer good for anything, except to be thrown out and trampled by men.
¹⁴"You are the light of the world. A city on a hill cannot be hidden.
¹⁵Neither do people light a lamp and put it under a bowl. Instead they put it on its stand, and it gives light to everyone in the house. ¹⁶In the same way, let your light shine before men, that they may see your good deeds and praise your Father in heaven."

"No doubt those listening to Jesus lived in rural communities. They were familiar with what darkness really meant, and with the significance of a city set on a hill. Perhaps they instinctively thought of the city set on the hill as Jerusalem. It gave light because it was the centre of their faith. Jesus gave that fact a dramatic twist when he said that he – not Jerusalem – was the light of the world, and his disciples were to share in that mission."

– Sinclair Ferguson

It Can Be Done: the real heroes of the inner city, Fred Catherwood, Lutterworth Press

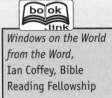

Windows on the World from the Word, Ian Coffey, Bible Reading Fellowship

The King's community – light of the world

Jesus describes himself in John 8:12 as "the light of the world" but makes it clear that this only remained true while he was in the world (John 9:5). The remarkable privilege and responsibility of the church is that we have now been commissioned to be the light. Once again we see that the statement "Don't look at the church, look at Jesus" flies in the face of his teaching.

This metaphor is a helpful description for the church, because light:

● **Illuminates** – a call to safety. In the absolute darkness of the Galilean countryside, the distant lights of a hilltop city would be a welcome sight (Matt 4:16). The church is to be a community that is a lighthouse of rescue to those that the Bible describes without hesitation as 'lost' (Luke 19:10) and 'blinded' (2 Cor 4:4).

● **Enlivens** – expressing life and energy. Light is dynamic – and the absence of light brings numbing cold and ultimately death. The followers of the King are called to be a carnival people, bringing life and colour to a monochrome world (John 1:4).

● **Exposes** – light reveals that which is in the darkness. The church has a prophetic calling to proclaim, but not legislate, the loving order and moral definition that God wills for humanity. This exposing light may create a reaction among those who prefer the cover of darkness (John 3:19).

● **Reveals** – As good works flow, so the spotlight of attention and 'glory' is placed upon the Father in heaven. He is revealed through his people. One translation of the word 'glorify' (*doxazo* in Greek) is 'to render excellent.'

Jesus amplifies this picture with the statement that a city set of a hill cannot be hidden. The lights of a city can be seen from a great distance – and may be a welcome sight to a traveller.

The King's community – salt of the earth

Salt was commonly used in New Testament times as a preservative, a flavour and also as a sign of peace in the making of covenants. Obviously salt must have a distinctive flavour – otherwise it is useless. As Luke, in his amplified version of the saying, puts it: "It is fit neither for the soil nor for the manure heap" (Luke 14:35). Jesus may have meant it was no good for the land, not even as manure.

REBUILD
Connecting church and community

More and more churches want to respond to the needs in their communities, but the expertise is not always to hand. That's why sixty national church groups and agencies have come together behind Rebuild, with a vision to help local churches make a lasting difference in their communities.

Whether your church wants to run a community project, to support your local schools or to learn how to be good neighbours, Rebuild can get you talking to another church doing the same sort of thing. Or they can point you to a Christian agency that has the resources to help you do the job.

You can learn from their experience and find out what works and what doesn't without having to make big mistakes.

National Community Week 21–28 July 2001: an invitation to do more

National Community Week is a way for churches to take the next step to getting involved in social action locally. National Community Week is an invitation to churches to commit up to one week of their time to do something concrete in their community.

You can choose from a big menu of inventive ideas for your church's Community Week, and Rebuild will put you in touch with the people who can get you started.

An example: A community church in Eastbourne was planning to launch a Care and Repair scheme. Working with a Rebuild coalition member, The Shaftesbury Society, and running the scheme as a Community Week gave them the confidence to get started and helped shape their long-term plans.

What is Rebuild?

Rebuild is a coalition of national church groups and agencies. They want to motivate local congregations to get involved in their neighbourhoods. Rebuild will help churches get moving by showing them what they can do, where the best resources are, and how they can learn from others who have 'been there, done that'.

What can you do?

Spring Harvest guests can:

- Visit the Rebuild stand at the Spring Harvest Resource Centre.
- Visit the Rebuild web site at www.rebuild.org.uk to find out more, and discover a wide range of links.
- Phone Rebuild on 0870 3300 212 if you need help with some aspect of community involvement.
- Plan to take part in National Community Week, 21-28 July, 2001 and start to make a difference in your community. (Some churches may want to choose a different date.)

Rebuild, c/o 16 Kingston Road, London SW19 1JZ
020 8239 5581
email: info@rebuild.org.uk
web: www.rebuild.org.uk

PECAN

The Peckham Evangelical Churches Action Network – Pecan – has played a big part in the government's New Deal programme in Southwark, and is working now on the new 'employment action zone' there. It started 10 years ago, providing training for unemployed people. Most people in the area live on one very large council estate, and few are there by choice. The recruiters knocked on every door to invite people onto employment preparation courses. They have been doing so ever since. Two or three times a year, they take the time and trouble to go out after people, to meet them and get to know them, not just waiting for them to come into the office. That is, after all, the approach Jesus took.

Thousands have been on these courses, and employment prospects in Peckham have been transformed. Most of the staff are recruited from the local churches and therefore have a knowledge of the area and the specific challenges it faces. All earn the same wage. Pecan is seen as part of the churches' work, and it is from the lives of those churches that it draws its inspiration and its determination. The result has been impressive change – the kind that the government wants to see in many other places, too.

Matthew 6

¹"Be careful not to do your 'acts of righteousness' before men, to be seen by them. If you do, you will have no reward from your Father in heaven.

²"So when you give to the needy, do not announce it with trumpets, as the hypocrites do in the synagogues and on the streets, to be honoured by men. I tell you the truth, they have received their reward in full. ³But when you give to the needy, do not let your left hand know what your right hand is doing, ⁴so that your giving may be in secret. Then your Father, who sees what is done in secret, will reward you."

"Whatever you do, work at it with all your heart, as working for the Lord, not for men, since you know that you will receive an inheritance from the Lord as a reward. It is the Lord Christ you are serving."

– Col 3:23–24

book.link

Love Must be Tough, James Dobson, Kingsway

"For you know the grace of our Lord Jesus Christ, that though he was rich, yet for your sakes he became poor, so that you through his poverty might become rich."

– 2 Cor 8:9

Matthew says, "It is no longer good for anything, except to be thrown out and trampled by men" (Matt 5:13). That is to say, people throw the useless stuff out into the street. The figure of insipid salt appears in the words of the rabbis, with reference (it seems) to Israel's role as the salt or purifying agency among the nations of mankind. Matthew's version of Jesus' saying begins with the words "You are the salt of the earth" (Matt 5:13). It is addressed to his disciples. This implies that the disciples have a particular function to perform on earth, and that, if they fail to perform it, they might as well not exist, for all the good they will do.

The church is therefore called to be a community that:

● Acts as a preservative in a decaying culture. The presence of authentic followers of Jesus who quietly live for the kingdom can slow down and prevent the deterioration that is inevitable when society as a whole rejects God's values

● Provides flavour – the distinctive 'taste' of God's alternative kingdom. The church is called to be both culturally relevant and distinctive in her own culture – a balancing act that is difficult to achieve. An example of this is found in our personal communication: "Let your conversation be always full of grace, seasoned with salt," Paul writes to the Colossians (Col 4:6)

● Demonstrates the peace and reconciliation that comes with God's reign. God invites us to enjoy 'kingdom relationships' rather than – to quote Roger Forster – 'Christianised friendships.' "Have salt in yourselves, and be at peace with each other." (Mark 9:50) This might refer to the eating of salt together, which was an expression of fellowship at the table and therefore of peaceful relationships.

Salt: incarnation, not quick fixes

Salt must be thoroughly mixed into the food that it will flavour or preserve. A church that tries to keep the world at a distance is therefore useless. Rebecca Manley Pippert captured this idea by titling her book on evangelism *Out of the Saltshaker*. Jesus came among us. In order to identify with and rescue us, he "lived for a while among us" (John 1:14). His world changing incarnation is our model for change.

The incarnate church:

● will encourage her members to be thoroughly involved with the real world beyond the doors of the church building. The church that spends most of its time hiding behind its walls,

THE KING'S COMMUNITY

BETHANY TRUST

The Bethany Trust works with homeless people in Edinburgh. Its director, Alan Berry, was a minister in a nearby inner city Baptist church. Confronted with Edinburgh's homelessness, he and three others set up the trust and bought their first property, to be used as a hostel for the homeless, in 1983. It now has about 80 full-time and volunteer staff, and accommodation for over 120. Everyone they work with knows it is a Christian project. They don't take the initiative in proselytising, but they are ready to explain their faith if they are asked. From time to time, they are accused of brainwashing by former residents. Ten years ago – in response to one such accusation – the city's Social Work Department mounted a major investigation, and concluded that the allegations were unfounded. The city council acknowledges that the trust is too big to ignore and that it is providing vital and high-quality services.

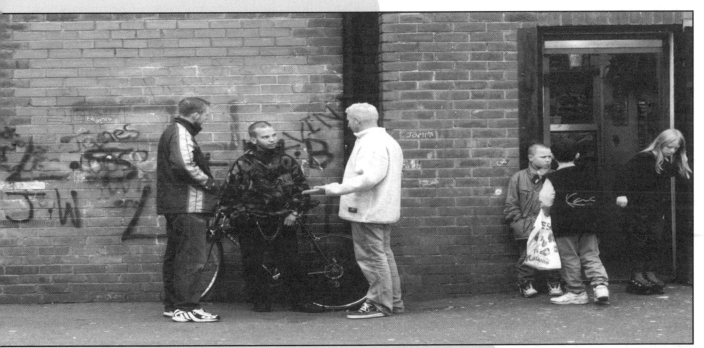

King
of the hill

Matthew 5

¹⁷"Do not think that I have come to abolish the Law or the Prophets; I have not come to abolish them but to fulfil them. ¹⁸I tell you the truth, until heaven and earth disappear, not the smallest letter, not the least stroke of a pen, will by any means disappear from the Law until everything is accomplished. ¹⁹Anyone who breaks one of the least of these commandments and teaches others to do the same will be called least in the kingdom of heaven, but whoever practices and teaches these commands will be called great in the kingdom of heaven. ²⁰For I tell you that unless your righteousness surpasses that of the Pharisees and the teachers of the law, you will certainly not enter the kingdom of heaven."

Asian Tigers for Christ,
Michael Green, SPCK

"The people who least live the creeds are not seldom the people who shout loudest about them. The paralysis which affects the arms does not, in these cases, interfere with the tongue."
"That which a person believes, they live by. All the rest is religious froth."

– unknown

only occasionally emerging for a brief evangelistic sortie will make little impact. The church that relies on large crusade-type proclamation or the mass distribution of literature, will be ineffective. *We* are called to be an incarnated people – and not just those who 'incarnate' mail in our neighbours' letter-boxes.

● is a serving church – in both attitude and long term commitment. She will reject quick-fix projects (that can make us feel better but actually accomplish little), or projects that are hastily organised and quickly completed.

● will demonstrate her priorities by the way that she spends her time. Are we too busy holding church services where we *talk* about changing the world to actually change the world?

● will encourage her members to realise that God's call will come to some of us to deliberately choose to live in areas where we can identify with and build friendship with the poor.

● will be aware of 'evangelical lift' – the upward mobility that tends to come to those who decide to follow Christ, so "the churches of the poor all become middle class churches sooner or later" (H.Richard Niebuhr). Christians do with time tend to prosper materially – this may be due to increased faithfulness at work, more careful stewardship of money and a new concern for education.

"The need, therefore, is not for expensive, large scale programmes to carry the gospel to the poor. The need is for ordinary committed Christians with the vision and dedication to work among the poor, to spend time with them, to live among them in some cases, to form, quietly and without fanfare, dynamic cells of Christian witness which multiply to transform the community for Christ."

– Howard Snyder

The King's community
– put away the trumpets

The church is called to naturally shine, and flavour – and by being that kind of people, to show the heavenly Father as 'excellent' – but she is not called to draw attention to herself. At first glance, this may seem contradictory. But the issue is found in our motivation: the Pharisees loved to be seen in their piety, so that they would be honoured by men (Matt 6:2). The church is not to act as an object of self-righteous admiration – our motivation is to see the Father honoured and glorified.

It was said of the early puritans that they lived their lives "as if they

PUT THE TRUMPETS AWAY

A ravenous hunger for the praise of men was the besetting sin of the Pharisaism. Jesus asked: "How can you believe if you accept praise from one another, yet make no effort to obtain the praise that comes from the only God?" (John 5:44) Similarly John the evangelist commented: "They loved praise from men more than praise from God." (John 12:43) So insatiable was their appetite for human commendation that it quite spoiled their giving. Jesus ridicules the way they turned it into a public performance. He pictures a pompous Pharisee on his way to put money into the special box at the temple or synagogue, or to take a gift to the poor. In front of him march the trumpeters, blowing a fanfare as they walk, and quickly attracting a crowd. "They pretended, no doubt," comments Calvin, "that it was to call the poor, as apologies (ie. excuses) are never wanting: but it was perfectly obvious that they were hunting for applause and commendation." Whether Pharisees sometimes did this literally or whether Jesus was painting in amusing caricature does not really matter. In either case he was rebuking our childish anxiety to be highly esteemed by men. As Spurgeon put it, "To stand with a penny in one hand and a trumpet in the other is the posture of hypocrisy."

– John Stott

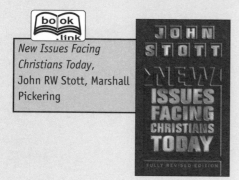

New Issues Facing Christians Today, John RW Stott, Marshall Pickering

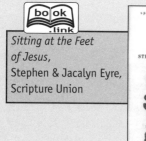

book.link

Sitting at the Feet of Jesus, Stephen & Jacalyn Eyre, Scripture Union

book.link

Streams of Living Water: celebrating the great traditions of Christian faith, Richard Foster, HarperCollins

"The truth of the matter is you always know the right thing to do. The hard part is doing it."
– General H.Norman Schwartzkopf

stood before an audience of One" (Os Guinness). They conducted their lives with the liberating motivation that, in a sense, the only person who had an opinion that mattered was God himself. So Paul tells us to work, "as for the Lord and not for humanity" (Col 3:23).

- As we live as those who stand before just **One**
- our works will be seen by **many**, and
- the **One** above will be glorified (see Matt 5:16).

⏸ Pause button
Are you cut off?

A strong commitment to following Christ naturally results in a deeper commitment to, and involvement in, the church. But over time, this can mean that the committed Christian is so involved in church activities that there's no time left to put many of these ideas into action. Are we too busy holding church services where we talk about changing the world to actually change the world?

We are salt and light. Pessimism and hopelessness do not belong among the people of faith. Do we believe that we can make a difference?

HALLMARKS OF THE KING'S COMMUNITY

Having looked at the big picture of the church, let's consider some of the specific radical hallmarks of this community that is to be a window to the world – a world that needs to see the effect of God's reign. Let's begin to focus on our own lives: the church can only be a corporate expression of what we are individually.

The King's Community – a people with integrity of heart

"Unless your righteousness surpasses that of the Pharisees" Matt 5:20

We will not consider in detail the relationship between the teaching

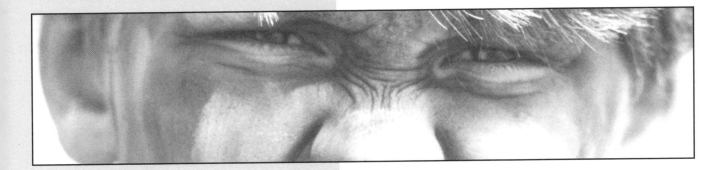

SIGNIFY LTD IS AN UPSIDE-DOWN COMPANY IN AN UPSIDE-DOWN KINGDOM

In the Sermon on the Mount, Jesus illustrates an upside-down kingdom. A kingdom that points to an inverted, upside-down way of life that goes against the social norm. Jesus set a standard that calls us to write a new script in every aspect of life. As a prophetic sign of the kingdom, Signify Ltd, a motivation and leadership development company, is seeking to write a new script within the corporate world, as an upside-down company.

"In today's society, securing your foot on the ladder of success, the motivation for power and profit, and the pursuit of security and wealth are treasured and prioritised by many. Signify's aim is to bring a new message into such a culture. The message is simple: 'Don't be satisfied with success,'" says Phil Wall, the director.

Through its products and services, Signify motivates and challenges people to fulfil their potential as well as bring significance to the world around them. The 10/10 Challenge, which is one such product, operates on the parable of the talents. Signify has applied one of the parable's principles by investing financially in the capacity of people to make a difference in their world. This is done in two main ways:

1. Giving £10 to an individual, challenging them to use their skills and abilities to increase it by 10 or 100 times.

2. Giving all profits made from the process to support AIDS orphans in Africa.

"Signify is an upside-down company," Phil says. "We don't exist to be successful and make profit for profit's sake. We want to go beyond success and use the company's profit to bring significance to those infected or affected by HIV/AIDS in Africa. We aim to break down the unhelpful divide between corporate success and charitable endeavour. Through the 10/10 Challenge, we add value to organisations by developing teams of people and by doing so impact one of the greatest social challenges of our day."

The company began with the aspirations of Phil and his wife, Wendy, to adopt an AIDS baby from South Africa, the child of a prostitute dying of AIDS. After seven months of effort and anguish, they discovered that this was not going to be possible. Thus they committed themselves to try and create a movement of people that would strive to adopt the AIDS orphans of Sub-Saharan Africa. With a task so great, a new script was going to be needed. The 10/10 Challenge is one response to their vision.

The 10/10 Challenge was originally run as Hope 10/10 – a project that Phil pioneered in 1998. With its strong focus on motivation and development, the 10/10 Challenge is well placed to run alongside other motivational products in his new company, Signify. The 10/10 Challenge has been presented in both voluntary and corporate sectors and has a track record second-to-none. To date, the 10/10 Challenge has given away over £140,000 to over 14,000 people and seen over a four-fold return of 600k.

Pioneer, Youth For Christ, The Salvation Army, Soul Survivor, Ernst and Young Financial Management, The Gallup Organization, and Hawthorne Savings Bank (USA) have all taken up the 10/10 Challenge.

W: www.bsignificant.com E: info@bsignificant.com
T: + 44 (0) 20 8241 2017 F: + 44 (0) 20 8286 4512

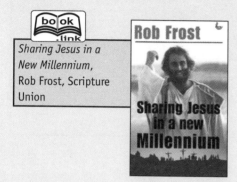

book.link

Sharing Jesus in a New Millennium, Rob Frost, Scripture Union

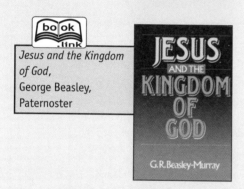

book.link

Jesus and the Kingdom of God, George Beasley, Paternoster

"The hallmark of evangelicals is not so much an impeccable set of words as a submissive spirit, namely their *a priori* resolve to believe and obey whatever Scripture may be shown to teach. They are committed to Scripture in advance, whatever it may later be found to say. They claim no liberty to lay down their own terms for belief and behaviour. They see this humble and obedient stance as an essential implication of Christ's lordship over them."

of Jesus to the Old Testament law (*see theo.link*). But let's deal with whether Jesus is demanding, in his call for a righteousness that surpasses that of the Pharisees, that we re-engage all of the details of the Mosaic law in order to follow him.

The answer is emphatic – no! Consider Paul's response to such a proposal:

Rom 3:20–22:

> "Therefore no one will be declared righteous in his sight by observing the law; rather, through the law we become conscious of sin. But now a righteousness from God, apart from law, has been made known, to which the Law and the Prophets testify. This righteousness from God comes through faith in Jesus Christ to all who believe."

Rom 7:4:

> "So, my brothers and sisters, you also died to the law through the body of Christ, that you might belong to another, to him who was raised from the dead, in order that we might bear fruit to God."

Rom 10:4:

> "Christ is the end of the law so that there may be righteousness for everyone who believes."

Gal 2:16:

> "Know that a man is not justified by observing the law, but by faith in Jesus Christ. So we, too, have put our faith in Christ Jesus that we may be justified by faith in Christ and not by observing the law, because by observing the law no one will be justified."

Gal 3:25:

> "Now that faith has come, we are no longer under the supervision of the law."

Jesus is calling for a righteousness that far exceeds – that is deeper than – the legalistic rules and regulations of the Pharisees. A righteousness that:

● **Goes beyond our heads**

The Pharisees loved to loudly debate and discuss doctrine. Theoretical orthodoxy was very important to them – and should be to us. But Jesus calls to us to a life that transcends mere intellectual orthodoxy – doctrine that goes further than our minds. He is calling us away from a righteousness that is, as one writer

JESUS AND THE LAW

Jesus said that he did not come to abolish the Law or the Prophets (the Old Testament) but to fulfil them. The theme of fulfilment runs through the New Testament and it is especially drawn out in Matthew's Gospel. Matthew shows how Jesus fulfilled each of these three views of the Old Testament and in turn shows us how to understand the Old Testament.

Jesus fulfils salvation-history

Matthew begins his gospel not with the birth of Jesus but by summarising the Old Testament story in terms of Jesus' ancestry (Matt 1:1-17). For Matthew, the Old Testament tells the story which Jesus completes. As we read the Old Testament it makes a difference to know that it leads to Jesus and that he gives meaning to it. How might we understand the Old Testament in the light of the fact that Jesus completes the story?

First, the reality of the Old Testament story is affirmed. The Old Testament is more than just a prediction about Jesus. It is the story of the acts of God in human history. ... stories about a true, real relationship between God his people. ... For example, the story of the Exodus tells us about his care for the oppressed, the poor and the suffering. It tells of his action for justice on behalf of the exploited. It tells us of a God of redemption who set his people free.

Secondly, Jesus sheds light backwards on the story. We understand a story in the light of its destination. The Old Testament cannot be fully understood without Jesus. Jesus once said to the Pharisees, who knew their Old Testaments in the utmost detail, "You diligently study the Scriptures because you think that by them you possess eternal life. These are the Scriptures that testify about me, yet you refuse to come to me to have life." (John 5:39–40) As St Augustine of Hippo put it, "The new is in the old concealed. The old is in the new revealed."

Thirdly, the Old Testament story helps us gain a full understanding of Christ. Just as it is possible to watch the last act of a play and get a great deal out of it, so it is possible to read the New Testament on its own. However, it helps to watch the earlier acts of the play as well if we are going to understand the climax and conclusion. In order to understand Jesus we need to read the earlier acts of God in our salvation-history.

Jesus fulfils God's promise

As we have seen, another way to look at the Old Testament is in terms of promise. In the Christian Bible, the Old Testament ends with prophecy, because the early Christians saw the Old Testament as a promise which Jesus fulfilled.

Jesus is not only the completion of the Old Testament story at any historical level, he is also the fulfilment of the Old Testament at the level of promise.

Jesus fulfils God's law

The third way to look at the Old Testament is in terms of law. Indeed, we have seen that Jesus himself refers to the Old Testament as "the Law" (Matt 5:18). In his prologue Matthew shows that Jesus fulfils the Old Testament story (Matt 1:1–17), and in the next section he shows that Jesus fulfils the Old Testament promise (Matt 1:18–4:14). In the Sermon on the Mount he shows that Jesus fulfils the Old Testament by revealing the full depth and meaning of the Old Testament law.

It is a mistake to think that the Old Testament itself is legalistic or that Jesus repudiated the Old Testament law. What he attacked in the Sermon on the Mount was scribal misinterpretation of the law.

The scribes and Pharisees had found 248 commands and 365 prohibitions in the Old Testament. In the Mishnah and the Talmud, which embody Jewish oral law, they added their own interpretation of these laws, in order to put a hedge of protection around the law and to avoid any possible transgression.

Jesus says in these verses that he has not come to abolish the Old Testament law, rather he has come to fill it out and to reveal the full depth of its meaning. He shows what the law means in terms of anger, lust, fidelity, integrity and care for others. He called his disciples to a righteousness that surpassed that of the scribes and Pharisees (Matt 5:20). He was not contradicting the Old Testament, but going in the same direction. He was building on it and surpassing it, whereas the scribal misinterpretations were going in the opposite direction in that they led to legalism.

So Jesus fulfilled the Old Testament law by showing us what it really meant. He also fulfilled the law in the sense that he lived it out. He is the only person who has ever done this, because only he has ever lived a sinless life. As German theologian Dietrich Bonhoeffer said about Jesus and the Old Testament laws, "He has in fact nothing to add except this, that he keeps them." He lived a righteous life. His righteousness far exceeded that of the scribes and the Pharisees. He showed us how to live a righteous life.

But he did not leave us there. He also fulfilled the law in that he made it possible for us to live a righteous life. Through his death and resurrection he set us free from the power of sin and provided for us a righteousness that comes from God (Rom 3:21–26). He enabled the Spirit of God to be poured out.

What the law was powerless to do in that it was weakened by the sinful nature, God did by sending his own Son in the likeness of sinful humanity to be a sin offering. And so he condemned sin in our sinful nature, in order that the righteous requirements of the law might be fully met in us, who do not live according to the sinful nature but according to the Spirit (Rom 8:3–4).

– *adapted from* Challenging Lifestyle, *Nicky Gumbel*

put it, "long on theology and short on charity, strong on the nouns of the Christian faith, and weak on the verbs." (see James 2:14–17)

- **Goes beyond our hands**

  The Pharisees weren't very good at doing what they believed. In some areas, they taught others but weren't willing to 'lift a finger' themselves (Matt 23:4). But a righteousness that exceeds theirs is not just about doing either. Jesus calls us to more than ethical ideals, or rigid moralism.

- **Springs from our hearts**

  The problem with the righteousness of the Pharisees was not just in their actions but in their hearts. It is a 'deeper' righteousness that is not just 'surface' behaviourism.

John Stott writes: "Christian righteousness is greater than pharisaic righteousness because it is deeper, being a righteousness of the heart. It was a new heart-righteousness which the prophets foresaw as one of the blessings of the Messianic age. 'I will put my law within them, and I will write it upon their hearts,' God promised through Jeremiah (Jer 31:33). How would he do it? He told Ezekiel: 'I will put my Spirit within you, and cause you to walk in my statutes' (36:27). Thus God's two promises to put his law within us and to put his Spirit within us coincide. … now it is this deep obedience which is a righteousness of the heart and is possible only in those whom the Holy Spirit has regenerated and now indwells. This is why entry into God's kingdom is impossible without a righteousness greater (i.e., deeper) than that of the Pharisees. It is because such a righteousness is evidence of the new birth, and no-one enters the kingdom without being born again."

The King's Community – a people with integrity of temperament

"Anyone who is angry with their brother or sister will be liable to judgement" (Matt 5:22).

Jesus never paints an idealised portrait of community life. His instruction is for the earthy reality of everyday life, which includes experiences of conflict, disappointment and tension. In fact, the church is bound to face relational tensions:

- Because of proximity. A church that goes beyond mere Sunday attendance encourages closer interaction, and that's dangerous!

Matthew 5
²¹"You have heard that it was said to the people long ago, 'Do not murder, and anyone who murders will be subject to judgment.' ²²But I tell you that anyone who is angry with his brother will be subject to judgment. Again, anyone who says to his brother, 'Raca,' is answerable to the Sanhedrin. But anyone who says, 'You fool!' will be in danger of the fire of hell. ²³"Therefore, if you are offering your gift at the altar and there remember that your brother has something against you, ²⁴leave your gift there in front of the altar. First go and be reconciled to your brother; then come and offer your gift. ²⁵"Settle matters quickly with your adversary who is taking you to court. Do it while you are still with him on the way, or he may hand you over to the judge, and the judge may hand you over to the officer, and you may be thrown into prison. ²⁶I tell you the truth, you will not get out until you have paid the last penny."

ANGER – 'YOU FOOL'

This is the first of a series of statements in which Jesus makes the requirements of the law more radical than the strict letter might indicate. Quoting the sixth commandment, Jesus says, "You have heard that it was said to the people long ago, 'Do not murder, and whoever murders will be liable to judgment'. But I tell you,..." he continues, and then comes the passage above, ending in the hard saying about the penalty incurred by one who says to another 'You fool.'

Murder was a capital offence under Israelite law; the death penalty could not be commuted to a monetary fine, such as was payable for the killing of someone's domestic animal. Where it could be proved that the killing was accidental – as when a man's axe-head flew off the handle and struck his fellow workman on the head – it did not count as murder, but even so the owner of the axe-head had to take prudential measures to escape the vengeance of the dead man's next of kin. Otherwise, the killer was brought before the village elders and on the testimony of two or three witnesses was sentenced to death. The death penalty was carried out by stoning: the witnesses threw the first stones, and then the community joined in, thus dissociating themselves from blood-guiltiness and expiating the pollution which it brought on the place.

Jesus points out that the murderous act springs from the angry thought. It is in the mind that the crime is first committed and judgment is incurred. The earthly court cannot take action against the angry thought, but the heavenly court can – and does. This in itself is a hard saying. According to the AV, "whosoever is angry with his brother without a cause shall be in danger of the judgment," but the phrase 'without a cause' is a later addition to the Greek text, designed to make Jesus' words more tolerable. The other man's anger may be sheer bad temper, but mine is righteous indignation – anger with a cause. Like the prophet Jonah, "I do well to be angry." (KJV Jonah 4:9) But Jesus' words, in the original form of the text, make no distinction between righteous and unrighteous anger: anyone who is angry with his brother exposes himself to judgment. There is no saying where unchecked anger may end. "In your anger do not sin," we are told in Eph 4:26; that is, 'If you are angry, do not let your anger lead you into sin; let sunset put an end to your anger, for otherwise it will provide the devil with an opportunity which he will not be slow to seize.'

There seems to be an ascending scale of seriousness as Jesus goes on: "subject to judgment. ... answerable to the Sanhedrin. ... in danger of the fire of hell." (Matt 5:22) The Sanhedrin were apparently the supreme court of the nation, in contrast to a local court. Evidently, then, to insult one's brother is more serious than

to be angry with him. This is clearly so: the angry thought can be checked, but the insult once spoken cannot be recalled and may cause violent resentment. The person insulted may retaliate with a fatal blow, for which in fact if not in law the victim of the blow may be as much to blame as the one who strikes it. The actual insult mentioned by Jesus is *raca*. The precise meaning of *raca* is disputed; it is probably an Aramaic word meaning something like imbecile but was plainly regarded as a deadly insult. (Words of abuse are above all others to be avoided by speakers of a foreign language; they can have an unimagined effect on a native speaker of the language.)

But whoever says 'you fool' is in danger of the fire of hell. From this we might gather that 'you fool' is a deadlier insult than 'raca', whatever *raca* may mean. For the 'hell of fire' (RSV) or 'hell fire' (AV) is the most severe penalty of all. The hell of fire is the fiery Gehenna. Gehenna is the valley on the south side of Jerusalem which, after the return from the Babylonian exile, served as the city's rubbish dump and public incinerator. In earlier days it had been the site of the worship of *Molech*, and so it was thought fit that it should be degraded in this way. In due course it came to be used as a symbol of the destruction of the wicked after death, just as the Garden of Eden became a symbol of the blissful paradise to be enjoyed by the righteous.

But was 'You fool!' actually regarded as being such a deadly insult? In this same Gospel of Matthew the cognate adjective is used of the man who built his house on the sand (7:26) and of the five girls who forgot to take a supply of oil to keep their torches alight (25:2–3), and Jesus himself is reported as calling certain religious teachers 'blind fools' (23:17). It is more probable that just as *raca* is a non-Greek word, so is the word more that Jesus used here. If so, then it is a word which to a Jewish ear meant 'rebel (against God)' or 'apostate'; it was the word which Moses in exasperation used to the disaffected Israelites in the wilderness of Zin. "Listen, you rebels, must we bring you water out of this rock?" (Num 20:10). For these rash words, uttered under intense provocation, Moses was excluded from the promised land.

Whether this was the word Jesus had in mind or not, he certainly had in mind the kind of language that is bound to produce a murderous quarrel. Chief responsibility for the ensuing bloodshed, he insisted, lies with the person who spoke the offending word. But behind the offending word lies the hostile thought. It is there that the guilty process starts; and if the hostile thought is not killed off as soon as the thinker becomes aware of it, then, although no earthly court may be in a position to take cognisance of it, that is what will be the first count in the indictment before the judgment-bar of God.

King of the hill

> "If you have been part of a local church for more than six months, and nobody has irritated you yet, then you're probably clinically dead."
>
> – Jeff Lucas

> "It is well established today that many people are killed by their own anger."
>
> – Redford and Virginia Williams

> "Rid yourselves of ... anger."
>
> – Col 3:8

> "When I am angry I can write, pray and preach well, for then my whole temperament is quickened, my understanding sharpened, and all mundane vexations and temptations depart."
>
> – Martin Luther

> "Anybody can become angry – that is easy; but to be angry with the right person and to the right degree and at the right time, and for the right purpose, and in the right way – that is not within everybody's power and is not easy."
>
> – Aristotle (348–322BC)

- Because of expectations. Christians are right to assume that the church will be better equipped to 'do' relationships – but we can quickly be hurt when expectations are not met.

- Because of principles. People of principle sometimes get confused about what is important and so become offended about issues that do not really matter.

- Because of the tendency to over-spiritualise conflict and 'dismiss' those with whom we have a disagreement. Most commentators suggest that the use of the term *Raca* (Matt 5:22) is a dismissive word that would be used to 'write someone off.' It was a word to express contempt – and may have originated from the sound made in the throat to collect spittle. Paul tells the Colossians, "Do not let anyone who delights in false humility ... disqualify you" (Col 2:18). This is a word that would describe the action of a football referee giving a player the red card and sending them off. One example of this would be when a group of people 'demonises' any that disagree with them and then leaves the church.

As we consider integrity of temperament, remember that it is not wrong to be angry. There is such a thing as righteous anger. Prophets and the psalmists speak of the anger of the Lord (eg, Isa 30:27; Jer 23:20; Ezek 8:8). For the rest of us too, there is a place for righteous anger. Indignation against wickedness is surely an essential element of human goodness in a world in which moral evil is always present. A person who knows, for example, about the injustice and cruelty of racism or the evil of terrorism or the sexual abuse of children and is not angry at such wickedness cannot be a thoroughly good person. Our lack of anger means a failure to care.

The difficulty we face as fallen human beings is making sure we do not sin when we are angry. Paul wrote: "In your anger do not sin: do not let the sun go down while you are still angry" (Eph 4:26).

Unrighteous anger creates a tendency to exclude, whereas Jesus offers an invitation to include. The fool, in biblical language, is wilfully perverted, rebellious and morally deficient. Proverbs describes him: "The fool is hotheaded and reckless" (14:16); "[He] finds no pleasure in understanding, but delights in airing his own opinions" (18:2); "As a dog returns to its vomit, so a fool repeats his folly" (26:11).

To brand someone a fool in this biblical sense was a violation of the

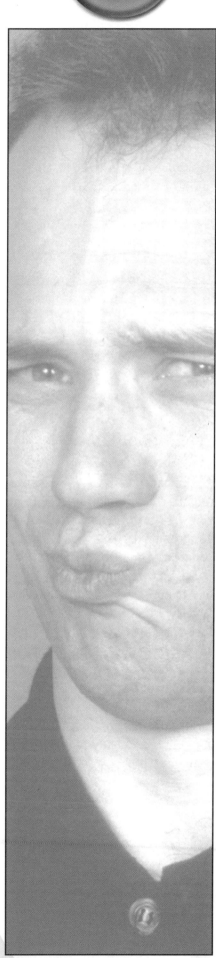

King
of the hill

Ugandan Bishop Festo Kivengere told how he was going off to preach after a row with his wife. The Holy Spirit said to him, 'Go back. Pray with your wife.' He argued, 'I'm due to preach in twenty minutes. I'll do it afterwards.' 'OK,' the Holy Spirit said, 'you go and preach. I'll stay with your wife.'
"The man who tells his brother he is doomed to hell is in danger of hell himself."

– Tasker

Matthew 5
²⁷"You have heard that it was said, 'Do not commit adultery.' ²⁸But I tell you that anyone who looks at a woman lustfully has already committed adultery with her in his heart. ²⁹If your right eye causes you to sin, gouge it out and throw it away. It is better for you to lose one part of your body than for your whole body to be thrown into hell. ³⁰And if your right hand causes you to sin, cut it off and throw it away. It is better for you to lose one part of your body than for your whole body to go into hell."

soul so devastating, of such great harm, that, as Jesus saw, it would justify consigning the offender to the smouldering garbage dump of human existence, *gehenna*. It combines all that is evil in anger as well as in contempt. It is not possible for people with such attitudes toward others to live in the movements of God's kingdom, for they are totally out of harmony with it.

So, when angry we need to:
● Watch our words
● Take the initiative for reconciliation
● Prevent escalation

Jesus presents images of a person turning the other cheek when hit, giving your coat to someone who sues you for you shirt and carrying the bags of a Roman soldier for two miles when he commands you to take them for one. These words should not be interpreted as new laws but as describing an attitude of kindness in the face of contempt and good that overcomes evil (Matt 5:39–42; ref overcome evil with good).

"These are attitudes that Jesus is describing in the Sermon on the Mount and are not to be taken literally. There is certainly no record that Jesus took them literally at his own trial. Literal interpretation will leave us with religion by regulation."

– Hugh Palmer

Pause button
A woman who had suffered sexual and physical abuse for a number of years was told by a fellow Christian that she "should not be angry, and just forgive". Is this good advice?

The King's Community
– a people of sexual integrity

"But I tell you that anyone who looks at a woman lustfully..." Matt 5:28

Murder is committed with words – and adultery with our hearts. The church has been remiss in not speaking with clarity on the issue of sexuality. Perhaps this silence is not so much the result of an embarrassed conspiracy, as a hangover from the negative heresy

INTEGRITY OF SERVANTHOOD

Most commentators seem to accept that in Matt 5:39 Jesus is not talking about physical assault, with the threat of physical injury, but about demeaning insult.

The significance of being struck on the 'right cheek' is that for a right-handed person to do this to you means giving a back-handed blow. This is less painful than a slap with the front of the hand administered to the left cheek with the full sweep of the arm behind it. It was considered, however, a greater insult.

This understanding of the verse fits in well with the two other examples (vv40, 41), which are also about people treating you unfairly, rather than threats of physical injury.

It is not about not passive, non-violent resistance. It is about responding with a spirit of generosity to those who mistreat you and don't deserve it. This does of course leave open an important issue. When does mistreatment become abuse that ought to be resisted, and what form should the resistance take?

– Ernest Lucas

THE WAR WITHIN: AN ANATOMY OF LUST

An anonymous Christian leader recounts his experience:

"I remember vividly the night I first encountered lust. Real, wilful commitment to lust." He describes how he was on a trip away from home and was lured into going to see a striptease show. "Ten years have passed since that awakening, ten years never far away from the presence of lust. ... I learned quickly that lust, like physical sex, points in only one direction. You cannot go back to a lower level and stay satisfied ... Lust does not satisfy; it stirs up ... where I ended up was ... incomprehensible to me when I started."

Although he never committed the physical act of adultery, it had a subtle effect on his marriage as he began to devalue his wife as a sexual being and focus on her minor flaws. It also had a devastating effect on his spiritual life, with lust becoming the one corner of his life which God could not enter. He felt torn apart by an overwhelming desire to be cleansed and an overwhelming desire to cling to the exotic pleasures of lust. Things came to a head when he went to visit a pastor of a large church and finally unloaded some of the guilt he felt, only to discover that this pastor had the same problem. Indeed, he took out of his pocket a pad of paper showing the prescriptions he took to fight the venereal disease he had picked up along the way. The lawyers were already dividing up his house, his possessions and his children.

– adapted from Challenging Lifestyle *and* Leadership Today, *Nicky Gumbel*

about sex that was perpetuated by the medieval church. It was widely taught then that:

- Married people were compromised because of their sexual relationship
- The Holy Spirit left the marital bedroom during sexual intercourse
- Monastic chastity was therefore preferable

Another problem has been the temptation to literalise the words of Jesus about gouging out your eye. When William Tyndale's English New Testament was published, there was widespread concern that "the whole realm would be full of blind men, to the great decay of the nation. … and thus by the reading of the Holy Scriptures will the whole realm come into confusion."

The most famous example of such painful literalism is the third century theologian Origen (185–254), who castrated himself. He later regretted his misguided zeal, and wrote that the words of Jesus should be understood "not according to the flesh and the letter." The Council of Nicea in AD325 passed an ordinance prohibiting such misguided surgeries.

> **The King's people are called to embrace an attitude that is far from an evangelical version of Victorian prudishness, which honours and celebrates the wonderful gift of sexuality in the liberating context of covenant – marriage.**

The tragic advent of internet pornography, and the rapid deterioration of any kind of restraint from the likes of Hollywood film producers, makes this call of Jesus ever more relevant.

So we are called away from:

- **Sexual superficiality** – where people become objects rather than human; where sex is separated from love; where 'attractive' people have the advantage simply because of their desirable appearance
- **A lack of self-awareness**. "If your hand or your foot causes you to sin cut it off," Jesus says – suggesting we should know whether or not it does. Different people have a variety of tolerances and vulnerabilities in their sexuality. What may be, for example, relatively harmless television for one person might be completely off limits to another
- **Mindless prohibition**. In the time of Jesus, a group of Pharisees

HELP FOR MARRIAGES

A selection of resources for married couples:

COUPLE ALIVE

from:

Family Caring Trust
8 Ashtree Enterprise Park,
County Down BT34 1BY

Tel: 028 3026 4174

KEEPING MARRIAGES HEALTHY

from:

Intimate Life Ministries
2 St Mark's Road,
Leamington Spa,
Warks CV32 6DL

Tel: 01926 421004

TIME FOR EACH OTHER

from:

Marriage Resource
CPO
Garcia Estate,
Canterbury Road,
Worthing BN13 1BW

Tel: 01903 263354

SIXTY MINUTE MARRIAGE VIDEO

from:

Care for the Family
P O Box 488
Cardiff CF15 7YY

Tel: 029 2081 0800

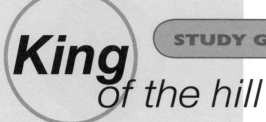
were famous for always walking around with their eyes tightly shut for fear that they might lust. They were called 'the bruised and bleeding group.' To admire someone and even to sense sexual attraction is not sin – it is the healthy prelude to, for example, marriage. The best translation of "look lustfully" (Job 31:1) is 'look with the purpose of desiring' or as one has put it, "desiring to desire."

- **Self-deception**. The mind produces rationalized arguments at great speed when lust is present. (We're just good friends, we understand each other, God has bought us together, everyone is doing it, and so on.) The adulterer is the one who would have wrongful sex if the opportunity presented itself – thus fantasy is ruled out. An even more subtle deception is that physical adultery is equally as bad as mental adultery – "If I've already looked, I might as well go all the way into the actual physical sin itself." This is blatant self-deception.

- **Careless eyes**. Jesus talks about the eyes and the hands. Job was aware that what he did with his eyes affected his heart, and so made a 'covenant' with his eyes (Job 31:1; see also 2 Peter 2:14 "eyes full of adultery")

- **Costless Christianity**. Jesus is calling us to take responsibility for our sexuality, and in those right choices to discover his help and grace. This call is in direct confrontation with the 'just do it' culture in which we live – and is a far cry from the 'let go and let God' idea that was popular in Christian circles for a while.

The King's Community – a people of marital integrity

Marriage is under fire. In 1994 in the United Kingdom there were almost 300,000 marriages and over 150,000 divorces – more than one divorce for every two marriages.

Some of the forces that contribute to breakdown of marriage are:
- An emphasis on rights rather than responsibility
- Unrealistic expectations of easy and sustained happiness
- The removal of parental support
- Acceptance of divorce and remarriage as an option
- Decline of religion
- Subtle media messages (via soaps, dramas & celebrity profiles) that a broken marriage may be sad but is inevitable

Matthew 5
³¹"It has been said, 'Anyone who divorces his wife must give her a certificate of divorce.'? ³²But I tell you that anyone who divorces his wife, except for marital unfaithfulness, causes her to become an adulteress, and anyone who marries the divorced woman commits adultery."

MIXED UP BRIDE?

In the Western world today, divorce has become normative. It is no longer seen as a tragedy, a last resort when all else has failed, but has become the first course of action as soon as a marriage faces any turbulence. The statistics for marriage breakdown are well known, with four in ten marriages ending in divorce. Fresh and disturbing evidence of the increasing prevalence of divorce was made public in October 1997, when Broken Rites, an organisation that seeks to help the divorced and separated partners of the clergy, made the astonishing claim that marriage breakdown among the Anglican clergy had risen to the same disastrous levels as in the rest of society.

Although this unwelcome statistic may indicate that in practice the church is now shifting to embrace the casual attitude of the school of *Hillel*, the official line of many denominations remains closer to the school of *Shammai*. It is very strange that in this sole instance the church has actually chosen to be stricter than Jesus, especially when it has specialised in turning a blind eye to many of the other radical demands of the Sermon on the Mount. Expressions of anger that Jesus condemned have become socially acceptable, but grounds for divorce that Jesus deemed acceptable have been rejected.

– Rob Warner

King
of the hill

book.link

Divorce and Remarriage, Guy Duty, Bethany House Publishers

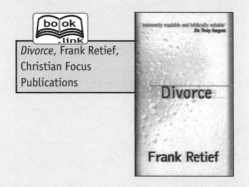

book.link

Divorce, Frank Retief, Christian Focus Publications

"And if your right hand causes you to sin, cut it off and throw it away."

– Matt 5:29

book.link

Divorce and Remarriage; policy options, Robert Warren, Grove

book.link

Growing Through Divorce, Jim Smoke, Harvest House

book.link

Breaking up without Cracking Up, Christopher Compston, HarperCollins

Trends in Marriage and Divorce

There are signs that the divorce rate has levelled off, remaining relatively stable at 13.5 per cent. Separation, however, is more common among cohabiting couples. Only 18 per cent of these relationships survive 10 years or more. Overall, therefore, the picture is one of growing instability among couples. Sequential cohabitation is accelerating the instability.

It is projected that by 2020 almost four in ten homes will be occupied by a single person. Government figures predict that in 2016 men under 65 will be the largest group living alone at 13 per cent of all households.

People still want relationships that last, they just seem increasingly unable to achieve them. A change in expectations is partly to blame. The new mantra is 'my partner must fit me exactly,' and if he no longer does I'll change him. New patterns of work are a source of conflict. When both partners work, and one is transferred, who sacrifices to be with the other?

One likely outcome is an increase in more direct and impersonal means of meeting potential partners – such as dating agencies and internet chat rooms – with the use of sophisticated psychological profiling. These agencies may also provide follow-up services and support packages to keep relationships on track.

By 2020, we could be surprised at the ways in which society has adapted to the changing nature of marriage.

– adapted from Tomorrow, *by Michael Moynagh and Richard Worsley*

Just as Origen mutilated himself because he took a falsely literalist approach, so there has been a great deal of misunderstanding as these words of Jesus have been interpreted as 'new law' or the sum total of his instruction about divorce. John Stott comments that the words of Jesus recorded here "seem to give an abbreviated summary of his teaching" and notes that these words should be read alongside a fuller teaching episode recorded in Matthew 19.

We tiptoe gently into this subject, recognizing that for so many today it invokes a deep sense of pain, loss and guilt.

THE ERASMIAN VIEW

Since the Reformation, the most common approach to the controversial divorce and remarriage issue has been the teaching first associated with Erasmus (known as "The Erasmian view", which he first taught in 1519). This view holds that:

- Divorce is acceptable, if one partner commits adultery
- The 'innocent' party may remarry
- If a Christian is deserted by a non-Christian, they can divorce them (the Pauline privilege of 1 Cor 7:15)
- In the case of desertion, remarriage is usually deemed acceptable.

King of the hill

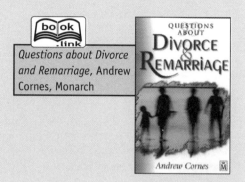

Questions about Divorce and Remarriage, Andrew Cornes, Monarch

"Some propose that those who have been divorced should return to their original partner and attempt to resume the marriage, even where one or the other has subsequently remarried. As a mandatory demand laid upon those who have been divorced, such an approach can only be described as tyrannous and irresponsible, cruel and absurd."
– Rob Warner

Whose side are you on? The context of the teaching

A theological war had been raging during Jesus' time. According to Rabbinic law a man had the right to divorce his wife, but the woman had no such right to divorce her husband. All that the husband had to do was to hand the document to the woman in the presence of two witnesses and she was divorced. As for the grounds for divorce, there were two different schools of thought, revolving around the interpretation of Deut 24, which appears to allow divorce when a husband finds 'something indecent' (v1) about his wife.

- According to the strict school, led by Rabbi Shammai, this meant a serious sexual offence
- According to the liberal school, led by Rabbi Hillel, the husband could divorce his wife 'for any and every reason' (hence the question asked by the Pharisees in Matt 19:3). This was taken to include gossiping in the street, losing her looks, having an unsightly mole or putting too much salt in his soup. Hillel's view appears to have been the more popular with men – and certainly the Pharisees leaned towards it.

So the question is put to Jesus (Matt 19:3): "Is it lawful for a man to divorce his wife for any and every reason?" In his reply, Jesus gives his view about divorce and remarriage (vv3–12).

The church has argued for centuries about the exact interpretation of these words, and we are not going to solve the problem in a few paragraphs.

What is clear (from Matthew Chapters 5 and 19) is:

- **Jesus focused on marriage – not divorce**. Referring back to the creation in Genesis, Jesus celebrates the divine origin of the marriage union. It is not just that man and wife form a social and economic partnership – they become one flesh
- **Jesus affirmed the sanctity of marriage** versus 'quickie' divorces. The destruction of the marriage bond is carnage in God's sight. Divorce is never God's ideal; but although he hates divorce – he loves divorcees as completely and compassionately as anyone else
- **Jesus upheld the rights of legally discarded women**. Legalistic men who divorced their wives for trivial reasons found no sympathy with Jesus. He called for women to be treated with dignity, not as objects to be sent packing on a whim with a red card. Divorce often meant social and economic ruin for a woman

– and the possibility of ongoing adulterous relationships

● **Jesus spoke to the issue of remarriage**: some suggest that divorce may unavoidable but remarriage should never be allowed, but Jesus assumed that remarriage was very likely following divorce.

● **Jesus recognized that the world is fallen**: "because of your hardness of heart." Some claim that divorce is always wrong and should be illegal, but Jesus accepts that it could at times be the regrettable but inevitable consequence of marital unfaithfulness. We affirm that Jesus is the redeemer who is able to enter even the tangled mess of our lives bringing grace, forgiveness and a bright future, regardless of the past.

Jesus stands between the extreme liberalism of a quickie divorce culture, and the extreme unthinking harshness of a church that forbids any possibility of divorce, or allows divorce but forbids remarriage under any circumstances.

Christians hold differing views on this sensitive subject. Care needs to be taken when expressing our own understanding about 'what the Bible says'. For many in our churches this is not an academic subject, but a deep personal issue with which they live daily.

The King's Community – a people of verbal integrity

"Do not swear at all, either by heaven, for it is God's throne; or by earth, for it is his footstool; or by Jerusalem, for it is the city of the Great King. And do not swear by your head, for you cannot even make one hair white or black. Simply let your 'Yes' be 'Yes' and your 'No', 'No'; anything beyond this comes from the evil one."
Matt 5:34–37

We live in a world where dishonesty is epidemic, where even Christians cover up their lies with the dualistic excuse 'business is business.' The police are caught red-handed framing suspects in order to get a result. Lawyers are branded professional liars, and politicians don't even really expect to be believed. We are not sure who to trust any more.

Jesus calls those who recognize him as King to be a different breed – a people who can be trusted and relied upon.

Matthew 5
33"Again, you have heard that it was said to the people long ago, 'Do not break your oath, but keep the oaths you have made to the Lord.' 34But I tell you, Do not swear at all: either by heaven, for it is God's throne; 35or by the earth, for it is his footstool; or by Jerusalem, for it is the city of the Great King. 36And do not swear by your head, for you cannot make even one hair white or black. 37Simply let your 'Yes' be 'Yes,' and your 'No,' 'No'; anything beyond this comes from the evil one."

Clement of Alexandria insisted that Christians must lead such a life and demonstrate such a character that no one would ever dream of asking an oath from them. "The ideal society is one in which no man's word will ever need an oath to guarantee its truth, and no man's promise ever need an oath to guarantee its fulfilling."

OATHS AND VOWS

Lynda Lee-Potter, writing in *The Daily Mail*:

The Sun newspaper recently conducted a 'truth searching survey' to find out more about the minds, hearts and integrity of its readers. It purported to be ecstatic to find only twenty-two per cent of them would kill a partner for cash, and a mere thirty-eight per cent of men would let their wives earn money as a prostitute. 'Congratulations' blazed the caring Sun, 'We have always known it, but now we have the evidence. You Sun readers are decent, honest, caring and trustworthy. You are loyal workers, faithful lovers, caring members of the community.'

'Except,' they should perhaps have added, 'those of you who are potential pimps or murderers.'

OATHS AND VOWS

Are all oaths and vows are prohibited to the Christian? (Matt 5:34) C.H. Spurgeon argued that a Christian should not take an oath, even in court. "Christians should not yield to an evil custom, however great the pressure put upon them; but they should abide by the plain and unmistakable command of their Lord and King." The Quakers have traditionally taken the same line.

However, it is not necessary to take the words of Jesus so literally as to exclude an oath in a court of law. Jesus himself responded to the oath of testimony at his trial (Matt 26:63–64). St Paul used solemn expressions to appeal to God (2 Cor 1:23; Gal 1:20; 1 Thess 5:27). The author of Hebrews wrote, "People swear by someone greater than themselves, and the oath confirms what is said and puts an end to all argument. Because God wanted to make the unchanging nature of his purpose very clear to the heirs of what was promised, he confirmed it with an oath." (Heb 6:16–17) The author could not have used this argument if he

had thought that oaths were sinful in themselves. Jesus is not outlawing, for example, the marriage vows. These are solemn vows which invoke God's name to underscore the commitment to the marriage.

We must not be pedantic in our interpretation of the words of Jesus, lest we fall into the same trap as the Pharisees. They took too literal an approach to God's words in the Old Testament and failed to see that what lay behind the commands was the need for honesty, truthfulness and reliability. The same desire lies behind Jesus' words as once again he goes back to the spirit and intention behind the Old Testament law.

The thrust of Jesus' words is that we should be people who keep our word. Jesus said, "I am the ... truth." (John 14:6) Christians should be known for their truthfulness, reliability and trustworthiness in their homes, personal relationships and work.

– Nicky Gumbel

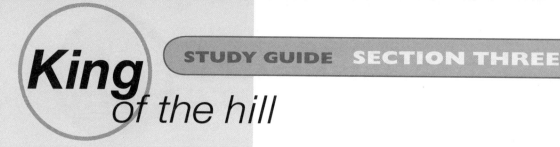
- This is not just about a legalistic refusal to swear an oath in court
- A call to such thorough integrity that people believe our word without the need for proof
- God does not need to be invoked or dragged into a transaction or a statement – he is already there.

Pause button
Verbal integrity

Is it possible that Christians who overuse the words "The Lord told me" could be guilty of violating the spirit of this teaching? What about our tendency to bring God into our conflicts? Experts in conflict resolution have said that their work is hardest among Christians because they have the tendency to "summon the Almighty" in the defence of their opinion.

Summing up

The King of the Hill calls for a community on a hill – full of light, full of flavour, yet pointing to God rather than itself. The taste and the illumination comes from its members being a people whose temperament, sexuality, marital relationships and speech are distinctive and different, because they are being changed from the inside out.

According to Jesus, people like this will be noticed. A city set on a hill cannot be hidden (Matt 5:14).

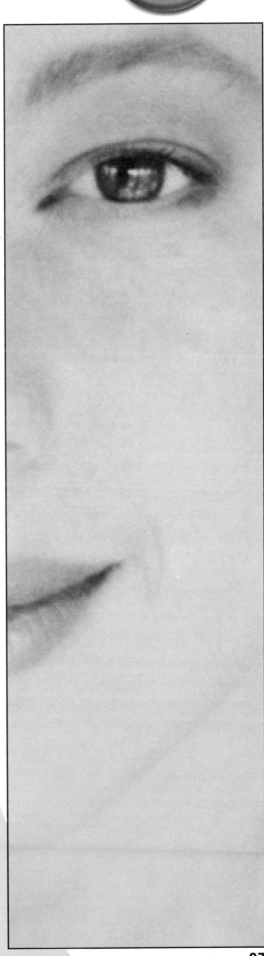

King
of the hill

BIBLE PASSAGE

MATTHEW
6:9–13

9"This, then, is how you should pray:

"   'Our Father in heaven,
    hallowed be your name,
10   your kingdom come,
    your will be done on earth as it is in heaven.
11   Give us today our daily bread.
12   Forgive us our debts, as we also have forgiven our debtors.
13   And lead us not into temptation,
    but deliver us from the evil one.'

7:7–23

7"Ask and it will be given to you; seek and you will find; knock and the door will be opened to you. 8For everyone who asks receives; he who seeks finds; and to him who knocks, the door will be opened.

9"Which of you, if his son asks for bread, will give him a stone? 10Or if he asks for a fish, will give him a snake? 11If you, then, though you are evil, know how to give good gifts to your children, how much more will your Father in heaven give good gifts to those who ask him! 12So in everything, do to others what you would have them do to you, for this sums up the Law and the Prophets.

13"Enter through the narrow gate. For wide is the gate and broad is the road that leads to destruction, and many enter through it. 14But small is the gate and narrow the road that leads to life, and only a few find it.

15"Watch out for false prophets. They come to you in sheep's clothing, but inwardly they are ferocious wolves. 16By their fruit you will recognize them. Do people pick grapes from thorn bushes, or figs from thistles? 17Likewise every good tree bears good fruit, but a bad tree bears bad fruit. 18A good tree cannot bear bad fruit, and a bad tree cannot bear good fruit. 19Every tree that does not bear good fruit is cut down and thrown into the fire. 20Thus, by their fruit you will recognize them.

21"Not everyone who says to me, 'Lord, Lord,' will enter the kingdom of heaven, but only he who does the will of my Father who is in heaven. 22Many will say to me on that day, 'Lord, Lord, did we not prophesy in your name, and in your name drive out demons and perform many miracles?' 23Then I will tell them plainly, 'I never knew you. Away from me, you evildoers!'

NOTES

King
of the hill

STUDY GUIDE SECTION FOUR

NOTES

THE KING'S FRIENDSHIP

THE KING'S FRIENDSHIP – MENU

We have been looking at the way Jesus' teaching in Matthew 5–7 affects our value system, our relationships and our church life. This session looks at the personal relationship we have with the King himself.

We will be challenged to think beyond the confines of simply 'prayer'. Nothing less than a life of closeness to him is the goal. We will want to re-examine our attitudes, priorities and lifestyle as our friendship develops with King Jesus.

King of the hill

Get a Grip on the Future, Gerard Kelly, Monarch

Threshold of the Future – Reforming the church in the Post Christian World, Michael Riddell, SPCK

Faith in a Changing Culture, John Drane, Marshall Pickering

"You sum up the whole of the New Testament teaching in a single phrase, if you speak of it as a revelation of the Fatherhood of the Holy Creator. In the same way you sum up the whole of New Testament religion if you describe it as the knowledge of God as one's Holy Father. If you want to judge how well a person understands Christianity, find out how much he makes of the thought of being God's child, and having God as his Father. If this is not the thought that prompts and controls his worship and prayers and his whole outlook on life, it means that he does not understand Christianity very well at all."

– J. I. Packer

THE KING'S FRIENDSHIP – HOLISTIC SPIRITUALITY

Over the last three days, we have considered the radical call of Jesus to his followers – a call that demands that we be a people who are distinctive and different in the quality of our lifestyle from those who do not follow the King of the Hill.

But this call goes far deeper than behaviour, belief, or good works – it is founded on a real spirituality – a deep love for and intimacy with God that avoids the pendulum swing extremes of:

● Liberal activism, which pursues kingdom agendas without the love and friendship of the King

● Privatized piety, which enjoys the King's presence and friendship without engaging with the King's concerns.

In short, God calls us to make friendship the foundation of our lives. Spirituality – an increasingly popular word in Millennium 3 vocabulary – is the pursuit of that friendship.

Wanted – a spiritual church that values truth *and* experience

"One of the key things that I hear people saying is that they think the church is irrelevant – they actually say it is unspiritual, that if you want spirituality, the last place to go to is the church. Many people seem to believe that the church is not a place where you find spirituality anyway. It's a place where you'll find hair-splitting theology."

– John Drane

There's little doubt that there is a grass-roots hunger in Britain today for spirituality and spiritual meaning. This is both encouraging and challenging for the church, because we must recognize that the hunger is for engagement with God (or any kind of spiritual force) rather than engagement with ideas and theories – even 'sound' ideas.

What is less encouraging is that many people today appear to be 'impressed with Jesus' but not 'attracted or inspired by the church.' Why do many give a clear thumbs up for God – and an equally clear thumbs down for God's church?

THE KING'S FRIENDSHIP

GRASS ROOTS HUNGER: THE FRENCH DISCONNECTION

With a long history of radical humanism and a public school system built exclusively and deliberately on the values of secularism, France might well be described as one of the world's least believing nations. All the more surprising then that belief in God, and in the nonmaterial realm, remains a strong and persistent feature in the lives of French young people.

In a nation in which weekly church attendance has plunged since 1945 from close to 80 per cent of the population to less than 14 per cent, young people cling all the same to a sense of God and an interest in spirituality. In 1994, the magazine *Phosphore 3* interviewed a representative national sample of fifteen-to twenty-year-olds to find out just how deep such beliefs run.

Their findings confirm that, while the church may be outmoded, God is in the house: 55 per cent thought the existence of God certain or likely, compared to just 38 per cent unlikely or impossible. And 40 per cent attributed the creation of the world to 'a greater power'.

Asked what they expected to experience after death, only 16 per cent believed that there was nothing. Among the rest there was belief in eternal life, reincarnation and bodily resurrection – but a full 50

per cent expressed the view that 'there is something but we don't know what'.

The *Phosphore 3* survey gave a clear signal that belief persists, but that it is less and less connected to traditional, established or orthodox creeds. Of the 55 per cent who rated the existence of God 'certain or likely', 31 per cent qualified this God as 'present within each one of us' while only 19 per cent could believe in God as 'a being who has spoken to humankind in history.'

Commenting on these outcomes, sociologist Francoise Champion linked the preference for an 'inner God' to deep cultural changes amounting to a new spirit of the age.

"What we look for today is personal experience," she says. "What counts is to feel something. This new way of dealing with faith is not restricted to the young."

Nor is it restricted to France – these findings resonate with parallel evidence right across Western culture. There is a blossoming of spirituality among the young people of Generation X and beyond, but for many this goes hand in hand with a rejection of the creeds of the established church. It is in this sense that the newly formed cultures of the twenty-first century are post-Christian.

– *Gerard Kelly,* Get a grip on the Future

THUMBS DOWN FOR CHURCH

"Before Christians get too excited about the renewed interest in religion," Mike Riddell writes, "it is well to note that the emerging culture's exploration of spirituality is in many ways a reaction against institutional Christianity as it has been experienced in the West."

John Drane sounds much the same warning. "Christianity is very firmly perceived as part of the old order," he writes, "and therefore something to be discarded rather than trusted for the future."

King of the hill

"We structure our churches and maintain them so as to shield us from God and protect us from genuine religious experience."
– Clyde Reid

"This hunger for spirituality does not today, perhaps for the first time in many centuries, cause people to come to the churches. If ... we live in the midst of a time of genuine spiritual search analogous to the Great Awakening, how do we communicate the riches of our spiritual heritage to a generation not interested in being in communication with what churches do?"
– Loren Mead

"We talked for more than an hour. He seemed to have been evangelised more often than Nicky Gumbel's hairdresser. 'I am incredibly impressed with the person of Jesus,' he confided, 'but there is absolutely nothing in Christianity or the church that attracts or inspires me.' I searched his face for a trace of cynicism. I found nothing but sadness there. I asked if he would help me build a church for people like him and he agreed."
– Pete Greig

"Is there any truth in the cliche that today's youth is fearfully searching for signs and portents, miracles, gurus and the big idea? Even the most ungodly clubbers now chill out to the sound of Gregorian chants and wear magic rune symbols on their chests."
– Helen Chappell

Church Next, Eddie Gibbs and Ian Coffey, IVP

Could it be that we the church have put such emphasis on doctrinal purity and prepositional concepts that we have at times swung away from the idea that God might be *experienced* as well as *perceived?* But we must retain **both** approaches if we are to avoid:

● **Unbridled mysticism** – spiritual experience which is not Christ-centred or biblically founded
● **Lifeless orthodoxy** – biblical clarity without divine encounter and friendship.

Our grip on doctrinal and scriptural foundations must be absolutely sure, lest we sink into a subjective quicksand of existential postmodern pluralism and mysticism. Yet our faith cannot be reduced to the mental adherence to ideas, as Jesus makes very clear in his most practical Sermon on the Mount. We need truth about God – *doctrine;* and experience of and friendship with God – *spirituality.*

An invitation to fly: the heights and depths of spirituality

Wallace Benn sums up the wonderful invitation to a living Christ-centred spirituality that is extended to all of us:

"The possibility of knowing Christ is similar to an aircraft flight. Sometimes, as the plane takes off, it flies through rain clouds at low level and the visibility is poor. But eventually the plane passes beyond the clouds and the rain into the sunshine. And it is totally different up there! God has given to believers the capacity to get to know Jesus better, to fly, as it were, at 35,000 feet in our Christian lives. Yet some Christians are happy to stay at 5,000 feet with the resulting poorer visibility of Jesus.

"Paul's aim was to know Christ better. He was not content with a testimony that only included what had happened when he became a Christian. Or even what the Lord had done for him last year. In fact, a Christian should be able to say what he has learned from the Lord yesterday. How rich our church fellowship would be if each member had an up-to-date testimony of his relationship with Jesus!"
– Wallace Benn, Jesus our Joy, Christian Focus, 2000

An invitation to live: whole-life, non-religious spirituality

One of the mistakes that we can make when we approach the subject of prayer, for example, is the tendency to isolate spirituality into a spiritual 'segment', or just a portion, of our lives. Jesus didn't

MYSTICISM

"I don't need theology or Bible teaching – just give me a friendship with Jesus."

The moment that we raise the issue of spirituality, we can swing pendulum-like away from the vital beds and banks of Scripture onto the vast ocean of subjectivism – ultimately leading us into mysticism. In some senses, the mystic and the evangelical are similar – in that both agree that fellowship with God should be our priority. The danger of mysticism is that scriptures are placed aside, and 'feelings' become the ultimate source of knowledge about God. Reason, intellect or understanding is scorned.

❯ Study, don't just meditate
❯ Keep Jesus centred – not experience
❯ Remember the work of Christ for you as well as in you
❯ Do not lose sight of the sinfulness of sin

PRAY TO IMPRESS

When it came to giving, some of the wealthy in Jesus' day announced their offering by hiring a trumpeter. His job was to herald their generosity on street corners and in the temple. Such a literal parade of human kindness seems preposterous and vulgar today. How could anyone be so self-centred and arrogant that even their giving became another pretext for self-aggrandisement and self-adulation?

While trumpeters have gone out of fashion, we have found other ways of making a public spectacle of our kindness. During TV-sponsored charity fundraising events, it has become customary to emblazon the names of donors across the foot of the screen. Others gather in the studio clutching outsize cheques waiting to announce their donation on camera and so obtain their thirty seconds of personal fame and public approval.

A century ago, the same desire for public display found expression through newspaper reports that listed the subscribers to particular charitable schemes. Like most excesses of the Victorian era such self-serving displays did not escape the scourge of Dickens' pen, notably in Mrs Jellyby and Mrs Pardiggle in Bleak House. Mrs Jellyby was so devoted to Africa that her children were constantly neglected. Mrs Pardiggle's proud boast was that her children's names could often be seen in public subscription lists, for she had persuaded them 'voluntarily' to give extensively to charity:

"My young family are not frivolous; they expend the entire amount of their allowance on subscriptions, under my direction."

As to praying, Jesus condemns standing in the synagogue and on street corners. It's not the posture to which Jesus objects. Nor is it really the location, since a synagogue and a street corner are perfectly reasonable places to pray. It is the motivation behind the praying for which Jesus has no time. His world was littered with people who, though they never spoke a word to God in private, found a sudden desire to pray eloquently whenever other people could see them. On the street corners their prayers were ostentatious, an elaborate and unmissable public spirituality that declared unmistakably to passers-by how very religious and devoted they were. The synagogue had degenerated into a place where such people went not to meet with God but to be seen by men.

Jesus sweeps aside such empty showiness as a blight upon true religion. I regret to have to acknowledge that I have sometimes met people who pray eloquently in public but never pray in private; people whose lives show little or nothing of living discipleship; people who make a great display of going to church on Sundays; people whose spirituality is all show and no substance. Jesus' warnings have by no means passed their sell-by date.

– Rob Warner

King
of the hill

"Whether the Indian tribes of North, Central and South America, the Aboriginal peoples of Australia and New Zealand or the pagan Celts of Europe, the religions of 'first peoples' are experiencing a remarkable, worldwide revival. Lecturer John Barry Ryan suggests some of the elements of native spirituality that appeal to the postmodern mind. 'These rituals are communal, earthy and experiential, with group involvement in rites that appeal to the senses,' he writes. 'This contrasts strongly with an individualistic approach to overly intellectualised worship forms that leaves the participant alienated.'"

– Gerard Kelly

"So it is that the human being can know about God, he can know about Christ's dying for him, he can even write songs and books, be the head of religious organisations and hold important church offices and still never come to a vital, personal knowledge of God at all. Only by the Holy [Spirit] can he know God."

– A. W. Tozer

"A ravenous hunger for the praise of men was the besetting sin of the Pharisees."

– John Stott

"Trumpets were blown when the Pharisees gave alms to the poor ... as a pretence that it was to call the poor ... but it was perfectly obvious that they were hunting for applause and commendation."

– John Calvin

"To stand with a penny in one hand and a trumpet in the other is the posture of hypocrisy."

– C.H. Spurgeon

approach spirituality in that manner – his prayer life was as natural as breathing – and he didn't teach prayer as a separate subject from the rest of the Sermon on the Mount. Jesus' teaching on prayer is entwined with and inseparable from teaching on:

- Hypocritical pray-to-impress posturing
- Materialism
- Forgiving each other
- Worry and trust
- God's Fatherhood
- Persistence in faith
- Practically applying what God says to us

This is a key point. When we segregate prayer in our lives, we can slip into irrelevant personal piety. The call of Jesus is not just to spiritual activity; prayer, fasting, and other disciplines of faith. He calls the crowd on the hill to a spirituality that is profoundly different from the popular approaches of the day, so embodied in the pretentious practices of the Pharisees. They could pray one moment and plot the death of an innocent man the next. Jesus calls us to a spirituality that is inseparable, woven into the fabric of our lives – and calls us to a spirituality that is, in a sense, 'non-religious'. This does not mean that we abandon all traditions, ceremonies, creeds and structured approaches to spirituality, but that we pursue a vibrant, living relationship with God.

Friends of the King: for his eyes only
Matt 6:1–6, 16–19

Religion is not a matter of style – it is a matter of heart. The Pharisees had developed a spirituality that was little more than a public parading of their piety – which Jesus roundly condemned. Loving the practice of prayer is not a sign of spirituality – according to Jesus, the hypocrites "love to pray" (v5). The Father is "unseen" (vv6,18) and so much of our pursuit of him should be in secret (vv4,6,18). The key points of the King's commands are:

- **Be careful in public** – Jesus doesn't condemn public gatherings for prayer and fasting, but posturing in those public gatherings. Are our carefully constructed public prayers heartfelt offerings to God - or theological speeches to make us look 'spiritual' to others?

- **Be careful about righteous acts** – good works are not condemned, rather the use of good works to gain applause.

- **Watch your motives** – to be seen (v1) and honoured (v2) by people. Compare this with the teaching from Day 4 about our

THE KING'S FRIENDSHIP

RELIGION AS STYLE

A superficial attempt towards 'non-religious' Christianity and spirituality will tend towards the abandonment of:

Liturgy – some would argue that it's done repetitively and so can become lifeless routine.

But liturgical worship can provide a doctrinal, rich, thoughtful and holistic experience of spiritual expression. And whether we acknowledge it or not, all churches have some form of liturgy – an accepted pattern of public worship that is relatively predictable.

Tradition – some would argue that, because it's been done over a long period of time, it must therefore be inherently flawed. Tradition can become an obstacle of meaningful spirituality – as Jesus himself taught.

But tradition itself is not wrong. It is traditionalism that can create a problem. (Matt 23:13 "Woe to you, teachers of the law and Pharisees, you hypocrites! You shut the kingdom of heaven in men's faces.")

Discipline – because it is possible for discipline to become legalistic slavery, the tendency is to reject discipline in favour of spontaneity.

But discipline is fundamental to the development of spirituality – the need to make clear, daily choices about the direction and priority of our lives.

Other people's approaches – the quest for non-religious Christianity tends to demonise the practices of other people while our own remain 'radical'.

But today's innovation becomes tomorrow's tradition. We are not in search of the ever new – but of the everlasting Jesus. The curse of mere religiosity is always ready to strike, whatever our background or denominational affiliation.

GETTING STARTED WITH PRAYER

Here are two ideas to get your prayer routine started. Alternate them to see which works better for you.

Write it down:

Take a sheet of paper and draw three horizontal lines across it, dividing the paper into four segments. Label the sections A C T and S.

In the first section, write a paragraph of adoration. List God's characteristics that especially move you today.

In the second, write a paragraph of confession. Specifically identify the sins that are on your conscience. (You may want to burn this paper when you've done with it.)

In the third, list God's blessings for which you are thankful.

And in the fourth, make your requests, whatever they may be.

Say it out loud:

A. Read or sing a psalm of praise or Bible passage.

C. Name your faults.

T. Express your gratitude.

S. Ask for help.

Keep it up:

Experiment with the routine. Adapt it to fit your situation, but be sure to include all four categories. Experience the blessings of balance. And see what God does in your life.

– Bill Hybels, Too Busy not to Pray

FOR HIS EYES ONLY
The Games people pray

Some pray like a BMW
Seven coats of shine and shimmer
Masking the hardness of steel,
With an Anti-Emotion Warranty
To guard against
The least sign of trust.

Some pray like a Porsche:
Nought to victory
In 6.7 seconds,
Banking on the promises
Of Pray-As-You-Earn prosperity.

Jesus recommended
Praying in the garage
With the door shut,
Engine and radio off,
Praying when no-one is looking,
Forgetting
The traffic of the day.
Meeting God in the quiet lay-by,
Far from the Pray and Display.

– Gerard Kelly

King
of the hill

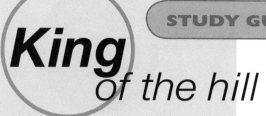

"If you went into the temple area at Jerusalem you would come into a courtyard. In the courtyard was a little room set aside, called the Chamber of the Silent. No noise or chatter was allowed there. When you had a gift to bring for the needy, you would bring it into this room and leave it there. After you had gone, the priest would come and take the money to distribute it to those who were most in need. It was a gift given and received in secret – no one knew how much you were giving, the priest didn't know who had put what there, the giver didn't know who would receive it and the recipient didn't know who had given.

"The Chamber of the Silent is a picture of how we are to give: in secret, not looking for any praise or reward, not making people feel 'beholden' to us."

– Stephen Gaukroger

Too Busy not to Pray, Bill Hybels, IVP

Rediscovering the Father Heart of God, Jeff Lucas, Crossway

www.24-7prayer.com

"It is even more pernicious if I turn myself into a spectator of my own prayer performance ... I can lay on a very nice show for myself even in the privacy of my own room."

– Dietrich Bonhoeffer

108

being a light on a hill, where people see our good works (Matt 5:16) and glorify the heavenly Father. The difference is – are we looking for God to be praised – or us? This includes financial giving.

- Note that Jesus says *when* you give, *when* you pray, *when* you fast. Jesus says *when*, not *if*. He assumed his followers would give, pray, and fast.

- Failure to guard ourselves from this kind of behaviour means that God will disregard what we do, because we have received our reward in full (Matt 6:5). The word used here described commercial transactions. The bill has been paid when we seek applause – no further reward or payment is due. We can even end up in the place where we seek to impress ourselves with our own behaviour.

- Faithfulness to this instruction will bring reward.

⏸ Pause button
Is it a good idea to publicly designate a group of people as 'the intercessors'? One writer says, 'true intercessors would not want such advertising.' Is he right?

Friends of the King: heartfelt sincerity rather than empty speeches Matt 6:7–8

If the Pharisees were guilty of pious performance, then the Gentiles were guilty of mindless babbling, which Jesus dismissed as a useless form of prayer and spirituality. Performance is a misuse of the purpose of prayer – and vain repetition is a misuse of the very nature of prayer – degrading it from a real, personal approach to God into a formula of words.

The enemies of liturgy should notice that repetition is not prohibited – but rather *vain* repetition. In fact, later in the Sermon Jesus exhorts those that pray to do so with fervency and tenacity – so repeated prayers are part of that process.

The Greek word translated 'babbling' (first translated thus by William Tyndale) is *battalogeo* and its original meaning is uncertain.

- Erasmus taught that the word is in dubious honour of the

REWARD

Reward is an obvious theme of the Bible, although we tend to be fearful that the idea of salvation by grace alone contradicts the idea of reward. But there is no difficulty so long as we insist that the reward is not salvation. This would be a serious misunderstanding: salvation does not come to us as a reward. Reward is something over and above our salvation. It is given to us in God's mercy as an encouragement for us to live for him. In the New Testament the theme explicitly begins here, in the Sermon on the Mount. A particular kind of life brings blessedness (Matt 5:3–12). Reward comes as we live for God alone, inwardly living for the 'well done' of God. Generosity to the needy is rewarded (6:34). Secret prayerfulness is rewarded (6:5–15). Fasting is rewarded, when it is done in God's will and as a means to serving him (6:16–18). It can never be wrong to live for God's reward.

(i) The reward has a lot to do with Jesus expressing his pleasure in us. It can never be wrong to seek honour from Jesus.

(ii) The reward is a spiritual thing. It is not necessarily something material or earthly. It can never be wrong to want Jesus to add to our spiritual well-being.

(iii) Jesus was a person who talked much about reward, and it is not possible to be more spiritual than him. The first step is to free ourselves from preoccupation with praise from each other, and fix our eyes on our Father.

– Michael Eaton

SURFING THE PRAYER WAVE

I really like the idea of surfing: The blue waves. The golden beach. The camper vans covered in cool stickers. The excitement of catching a wave...

So I stuck a 'pop-up' board on the roof of my Volvo 340 and drove down to Cornwall. On Fistral Beach the sea was flatter than a hedgehog on the M25. I joined the bleach-blond, beach bums sitting on the sand gazing longingly out to sea and dreamed about surfing. Perhaps I would turn out to be a natural. A born genius. Some kind of wonder-kid.

The next day as the waves picked up, I squeezed into a wet-suit, grabbed my board and waded out into the Cornish sea. I spent the next few hours utterly failing to stand on that bit of plastic. I flung myself about wildly, pursuing my little dream. But I utterly failed to surf. I wanted to do it. I just discovered I was bad at it. Appalling in fact.

So many people are committed to the idea of prayer. They believe in it. They know God is calling them to do more of it. But they find they're just bad at it. Young people especially find it difficult to discipline their spiritual passion into a daily 'Quiet Time' with God and often find the weekly church prayer meeting about as enticing as a trip to B&Q.

The **24-7prayer** movement started by accident when a bunch of students in Chichester decided to do something about their appalling prayer lives. We decided to try and pray non-stop for a month in a room, split into 1-hour shifts. And the weird thing is that it worked.

Suddenly people who were bad at praying found that it was easier to pray in a room where God was hanging out too. One hour felt like 10 minutes. Prayers got answered. New Christians thought it normal to pray for an hour. Artwork just exploded over the walls. We couldn't stop at the end of the first or second months. And in the third month the model just exploded around the world. We were totally surprised! Within a year there were 24-7 prayer rooms in 18 nations from Alaska to Australia. A web site linking the rooms just went crazy receiving millions of hits. The prayer meeting has now continued without a single break for 15 months.

People who are bad at praying are learning to pray. In fact they are praying like they have never prayed before. They are learning to make history through prayer. But more importantly, they are spending time alone with their heavenly Father, becoming more and more like him.

One of the dangers for the emerging generation is that we have a public cause without a private spirituality. 24-7 shows that the passion is there, waiting to be unlocked and released into a grey, grey world.

– Pete Grieg

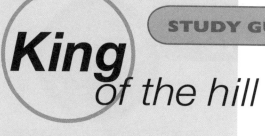

King of the hill

"Ultimately the only reason for pleasing men is that we may please ourselves."

– Martin Lloyd Jones

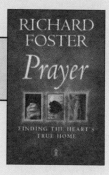

Praying With Jesus, Rob Warner, Hodder & Stoughton

"We should show when tempted to hide and hide when tempted to show."

– A.B. Bruce

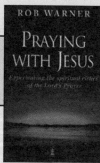

Prayer – Finding the Heart's True Home, Richard Foster, Hodder & Stoughton

Tomorrow: Using the Future to Understand the Present, Michael Moynagh and Richard Worsley, Lexicon Editorial Services

Cyrenean King Battus, who had a stuttering problem
- Greek scholars Grimm and Thayer suggest the word comes from Battus, an author of 'tedious and wordy poems'
- Most say it comes from the same root word as barbarians, which was used by the Greeks to describe the sound of a foreign language as being like stammering.

Jesus is calling us away from prayer that is speaking without thinking, as the RSV Bible puts it, "heaping up empty phrases", or as John Stott says, "All lips and no mind or heart." Ironically, it is likely no prayer has been 'parroted' more than the prayer that Jesus taught during his Great Sermon. This may be due to:
- Development of teaching early in the second century suggesting that Christians ought to recite the Lord's prayer three times each day
- Seeing the Lord's prayer as a prayer form rather than a prayer model. Jesus said, "this is how you should pray", not this is *what* you should pray
- John Bunyan taught that the Lord's prayer was a model and should *never* be used as an actual prayer, but perhaps he overstated the case. Why can't we use these wonderful words as both model and liturgy – remembering that, either way, they should never be used without thought in a mechanical manner.

Jesus affirms that:
- God is unimpressed by how many words we use in prayer
- God is the Father who knows us and our needs beyond our prayer habits.

Pause button
Of all the things in the universe that God could see as important, he asks us to prioritise this: talking with him regularly. Why?

Friends of the King: the Father beckons Matt 6:9
The Jews of Jesus' time preferred to use exalted titles for God, such as Sovereign Lord and King of the Universe – and so Jesus' instruction to use the word *abba* (papa) would have been shocking. But this is not optional teaching – the foundation of Christianity is the Father Heart of God. In teaching his disciples to say 'Our Father,' Jesus

HEAPING UP EMPTY PHRASES

At a practical level, we should be aware that when we pray in front of others, we can resort to:

Using out-of-date language
> *thee* and *thine* – though this probably has more to do with the Bible that we have read or were raised with than anything else

Cliches
> *travelling mercies* – I hope you get there safely
> *laid aside on a bed of sickness* – they've not been very well

Repetition of a keyword
> *just* and *really*

Volume
> anointing is measured in decibels

Trendy over familiarity
> calling God *pal* or *mate*

There are no rules – be yourself, but think about what you're saying.

THE FATHER BECKONS

He is inviting you – and me – to come home, to come home to where we belong, to come home to that for which we were created. His arms are stretched out wide to receive us. His heart is enlarged to take us in.

For too long we have been in a far country: a country of noise and hurry and crowds, a country of climb and push and shove, a country of frustration and fear and intimidation. And he welcomes us home: home to serenity and peace and joy, home to friendship and fellowship and openness, home to intimacy and acceptance and affirmation

We do not need to be shy. He invites us into the living room of his heart where we can put on old slippers and share freely. He invites us into the kitchen of his friendship where chatter and batter mix in good fun. He invites us into the dining room of his strength, where we can feast to our heart's delight. He invites us into the study of his wisdom where we can learn and grow and stretch ... and ask all the questions we want. He invites us into the workshop of his creativity, where we can be co-labourers with him, working together to determine the outcomes of events. He invites us into the bedroom of his rest where new peace is found, and where we can be naked and vulnerable and free.

It is also the place of deepest intimacy, where we know and are known to the fullest.

– Richard Foster

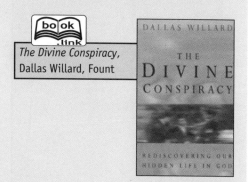

An article in *The Evening Standard* about the successful television and radio personality Chris Evans asked, "So why isn't this man laughing?" It went on:

"On paper, Evans ought to be a happy man. He is just 27, his Channel 4 contract was said to be worth some £1.5 million a year, he has several marvellous cars, a splendid new flat on Tower Bridge and a beautiful woman with whom to share it. But far from it, he seems quite depressed. 'It hit me one Sunday morning,' he explains, 'that all I ever wanted was the 10 o'clock Saturday night slot on Channel 4 and now I'd achieved my life ambition at 27. So what do I do next?

"'You can compare it to climbing Everest. You climb it, and what do you do then? Climb the north face? OK, but so what? And then? Climb the north face with a grand piano over your shoulder? There has to be more to life. Finding out what that might be is the problem I've had ever since that Sunday. I haven't got any closer to working it out.'"

extends a radical invitation to intimacy. He was not being merely sentimental here: His invitation shows us that the God we seek in prayer is:

● Personal – our father – not force
● More than the God of the individual – he is *our* father
● Loving – Papa without the childish connotations
● Powerful – in heaven (a phrase that expresses the spread of his royal reign and influence rather than simply his location)

The statement also encourages us to draw near to God in prayer, as a good father:

● Delights to spend time with his children
● Is upset when his children lie to him or read speeches to him instead of talking to him
● Receives his children freely
● Is personally affronted when his children shrink back from him in fear

Pause button

If this challenge from Jesus is taken to mean that prayer can never be reduced to heartless, impersonal formulae, then surely there is danger in the "Ten Steps to God's Blessing" approach of some in the so-called health and wealth/prosperity movements and churches. Whenever blessing is sought by spiritual laws or formulae, rather than by intimate interaction with God, are we not straying into preoccupation with the blessing rather than the One who blesses?

Friends of the King: his kingdom priorities rather than ours Matt 6:9ᵇ–10

The cult of 'me' is found everywhere: high street bookshops are loaded with books that market countless forms of 'spirituality' designed to help us become more:

● Self-aware
● Fulfilled
● Competent in relationships
● Efficient managers
● Able to break habits

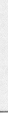

THE CULT OF ME

A churchgoer may embrace Christian values on Sunday, workplace values on Monday and consumerist values on Saturday. Sometimes there is disquiet at the inconsistencies involved. This disquiet will become less marked as the idea spreads that it is perfectly acceptable to adopt different values on different occasions. 'What works for me at the time' will be all-pervasive. So when I drive to work I may want better roads. Back home with environmentally conscious friends, I'll want better public transport. The inconsistency won't worry me, but framing public policy will be a nightmare! Should politicians listen to people when they are driving to work or chatting in the pub?

'It must fit me exactly', 'I want what I want', 'It's up to you' and 'What works is what counts' are emerging as the big stories that will shape people's values. So are we entering a thoroughly selfish world? Not necessarily. The individual's demand, 'I want', will be answered by the organisation which says, 'I serve'.

– From The Tomorrow Report: Using the Future to Understand the Present, *Michael Moynagh and Richard Worsley*

King
of the hill

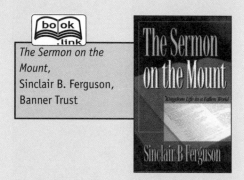

The Sermon on the Mount, Sinclair B. Ferguson, Banner Trust

"We must not be troubled by unbelievers when they say that this promise of reward makes the Christian life a mercenary affair. There are different kinds of rewards. There is the reward which has no natural connection with the things you do to earn it and is quite foreign to the desires that ought to accompany those things. Money is not the natural reward of love; that is why we call a man mercenary if he marries a woman for the sake of her money. But marriage is the proper reward for a real lover, and he is not mercenary for desiring it. A general fights well in order to get a peerage is mercenary; a general who fights for victory is not, victory being the reward of battle as marriage is the proper reward of love. The proper rewards are not simply tacked on to the activity for which they are given, but are the activity itself in consummation."

– C.S. Lewis

- Likely to meet goals and fulfil ambitions
- 'Successful' in life

But the spirituality of the kingdom does not start with the objective of our self-actualisation – it centres on the King's name, the King's kingdom, and the King's will. While it is true that Jesus meets our needs, we should be careful about presenting a gospel that primarily promises to:

- Fill the God-shaped hole within us
- Enable us to fulfil our dreams
- Meet our needs.

God has dreams he wants to fulfil – his dreams, in us. Our spirituality is not designed to make us better people, but to help us offer ourselves to the purposes and objectives of the King and the kingdom.

The Lord's model prayer shows us we are not to put a shopping list of our desires first, but concentrate on God's concerns. Perhaps this also helps us to have a sense of perspective when we do come to sharing our problems with God.

- May the name of God be 'hallowed' – let your name be treated as holy in my life, my church, and my world
- May the kingdom of God come – note the kingdom priority, hastening the day, as the kingdom comes daily. Asking for the kingdom of God to break out in every sphere of life
- May the Father's will be done – God's order and reign on earth, as it is perfectly established in the heavens. Asking the Lord to break into the chaos and disorder with his reign and rule.

Pause button
If God is so entirely sovereign that his kingdom will come and his will will be done, regardless of whether we pray or not – then why would he ask us to pray in this way?

Friends of the King: loyalty and materialism
Matt 6:11, 19–34

The Lord's model prayer moves into personal requests – and the first (perhaps surprisingly placed before the need for forgiveness from sin) is for daily bread. Tertullian, Cyprian, Augustine and Jerome

MATERIALISM

The Christian is not indifferent to eating, drinking, or clothes. They are necessities for living in this world and in society. But they are never his masters. He has learned that he does not need to eat in the most fashionable restaurants in town or cook the most elegant meals in order to live life to the full. Nor does he need the latest fashion in clothes to feel 'accepted' where it really matters. Jesus has taught him that 'life is more than food and the body more than clothes.'

Open a glossy magazine and read the advertisements. What do so many of them tell you? Life is centred on food, drink, and clothing. One can verify this by glancing through most glossy magazines. Almost without exception, the advertisements proclaim the virtues of food, drink, and dress in one form or another. Some advertisements even announce the brand of cat food that will make your feline friend look her best!

What has happened? The basic necessities of life – life's servants, as it were – have become our masters. But Jesus says, there is more to life than food. The person whose life is expressed through a body is far more important than the clothes it wears.

How, then, are we to think about these things? Jesus bids us to look at the whole of life. The birds of the air and the flowers of the field demonstrate what an exquisite designer and provider God is. If he provides with a tender, father-like care for these, how much more will he provide for the people he has purchased at the infinite cost of the death of his Son (Rom 8:32)? Can you not believe that the Lord will provide for you everything you need in your life?

– Sinclair Ferguson

THE FANTASY

Like Gulliver, the postmodern person is tied down into consumption by a thousand fine threads and is asleep. The ability to swallow a lie is one of the best indices of our ability to mess up, and we are now gulping.

The religion of consumerism flourishes only because the priests are well paid and the lies are not called: 'Do you want a recession, or something?' But it demolishes other areas of life or bends them to its service. Politics becomes consumption of the Clinton/Lewinsky saga or other mindless personal dramas. Religion and our life in relation to God are drowned in the sea of shopping. Do not go to church, but come to a supermarket. Morality and the good life sink beneath the life of goods. Surprisingly,

education, the commitment to wisdom, understanding, values, and learning are also easily defeated. Television as consumption outweighs the processes of learning in a child's life.

Consumption has such a strong hold over culture that it is culture. 'That painting's worth half a million.' 'The classics? Do they sell?' The inroads of the arms trade, drugs companies and many other ardent consumer enterprises into the structure of higher education are breathtaking. So there are, it seems, no independent areas left standing before the onslaught of this ideology of salvation by buying. Herbert Marcuse's *One-Dimensional Man* and one-dimensional living have arrived. But the consumption myth is not even remotely true.

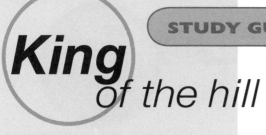

King
of the hill

"Today the heart of God is an open wound of love. He aches over our distance and preoccupation. He mourns that we do not draw near to him. He grieves that we have forgotten him. He weeps over our obsession with muchness and manyness. He longs for our presence."

– *Richard Foster*

Christ and Consumerism: A critical analysis of the spirit of the Age, ed. Craig Bartholomew and Thorsten Moritz, Paternoster Press

CHRIST AND CONSUMERISM

A Critical Analysis of the Spirit of the Age

"In one of their magazines, the National Secular Society (NSS) states, 'Nobody is listening: Christians who actually believe in the power of prayer are an odd lot. For the more they bow the head, bend the knee and grovel to their God, the worse he treats them.' They go on to write of '... this sado-masochistic relationship between the Almighty and his sycophantic supplicants.' "The NSS, perhaps not surprisingly, have failed to grasp what prayer involves. We approach a loving Father with boldness. We come to speak to heavenly dad. We don't need to grovel about in the dust. We are accepted by Father God and on that basis can enjoy praying to him."

– *Bill Hogg*

reacted against this emphasis on the physical by suggesting 'daily bread' is "the invisible bread of the Word of God" or Holy Communion – a notion Calvin dismissed as "exceedingly absurd."

God does not separate out spiritual requests from physical needs – but shows his loving concern for every area of our lives. Luther saw that bread is a symbol for "everything necessary for the preservation of this life, like food, a healthy body, good weather, house, home, wife, children, good government and peace."

A few verses later in the Sermon, Jesus gives teaching about treasure – the call to make God and his kingdom, rather than the false God of materialism, the centre of our interest.

We all have things we treasure, including:
- material goods
- reputation
- appearance
- human relationships
- security
- business
- country
- fame or significance

By teaching us to pray for daily provision, and calling us away from the lure of trusting in 'earthly treasure,' Jesus is not:
- Suggesting we should not work – rather that we should acknowledge and trust in the reality that God is our ultimate source
- Banning saving or insurance – Scripture praises the industrious ant, which stores for the future (Prov 6:6, 30:25)
- Making possessions evil – not that possessions themselves are wrong; but it is wrong when we are possessed by possessions
- Prohibiting the enjoyment of good things – God "richly provides us with everything for our enjoyment." (1 Tim 6:17)
- Setting up a treasury of merits for the afterlife – this is not a system for salvation, but a description of the lifestyles and values of the saved.

Jesus calls us away from materialism, which is:
- **selfish** – in a world where one third of all children die from malnutrition-related diseases before the age of five, and where one third of the world's people consume two-thirds of the world's

MAMMON

Mammon, an Aramaic term, means "wealth, money, property, or profit." The striking truth here is that Jesus sees *mammon* claiming divine status. In his view it competes directly with God. Wealth, more than anything else, can act like a god. Jesus doesn't grant deity status to knowledge, skill, appearance, occupation, nobility or nationality. It is wealth, he says, which clamours to control and boss us like a deity.

Fluctuations of the stock market can become our obsession. We easily become engrossed with new gadgets and begin serving them. As new toys captivate children, so material pursuits can captivate grownups. We bow down and worship at the altar of materialism. Luxuries begin to manipulate and dictate our lives. *Mammon* turns into a god. We can't serve God and wealth simultaneously. We can use wealth to serve God's ends, but that's quite a different thing than serving wealth itself.

– Donald Kraybill

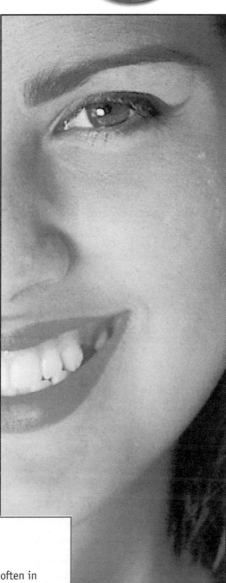

WORTH MORE THAN THE BIRDS

The second hindrance to the experience of joy is worry... . One of the reasons we worry so often in life is because we conclude we will be in a situation that we will not be able to cope with. But Paul reminds believers that the divine resources available to each Christian will not fail. Therefore 'do not be anxious about anything.' Since God's resources are available to us by his ever-present Spirit, why should we worry unduly? John Gwyn-Thomas wrote a great book on Philippians 4 called *Rejoice Always*. In his book he says this: 'The devil does not want us to bring our problems, great or small, to God, because he does not want us to see them in their proper perspective.'

Do you remember when you were growing up and measuring your height to see how you were growing? Sometimes we measure our problems simply by the size of the problem, or by other people's problems. But we should measure the problems by the presence of God with us. And if we measure our problems by God, he's always bigger than our problems.

Listen again to John Gwyn-Thomas: 'The answer to care is prayer.' And again: 'Every anxiety is a personal invitation from God to come before him in prayer, to call us back into his presence, to talk to him about it.' So every anxiety, every worry, potentially drives us to our knees and draws us into a deeper, richer fellowship with God as we talk to him about our worries and as we realise he's with us.

– Wallace Benn

King
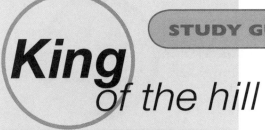
of the hill

"The appeals of consumerism are pathetic in that they are not true. Cosmetics claiming to give a natural appearance instead cover it up. So we have an invasion which landscapes the mind, emotions and inner character of millions of people, even though it is fabricated of lies. ... the consumption myth is not even remotely true."

– Alan Storkey

Faith in the Poor,
Bob Holman, Lion Publishing

"Jesus reminds us that prayer is a little like children coming to their parents. Our children come to us with the craziest requests at times. Often we are grieved by the meanness and selfishness of their requests, but we would be all the more grieved if they never came to us even with their meanness and selfishness. We are simply glad that they do come – mixed motives and all."

– Richard Foster

"The kingdom of God is his royal rule. As he is already holy so he is already King, reigning in absolute sovereignty over both nature and history. Yet when Jesus came he announced a new and special break-in of the kingly rule of God, with all the demands of submission which the divine rule implies. To pray that his kingdom may come is to pray both that it may grow, as through the church's witness people submit to Jesus, and that soon it will be consummated when Jesus returns in glory to take his power and reign."

– John Stott

resources, materialism insists we ignore the poor

- **fantasy** – promising everything and delivering little. Jesus states it clearly: "A man's life does not consist in the abundance of his possessions" (Luke 12:14)

- **temporary** – earthly treasure doesn't last. The word 'rust' literally means 'eaten away.' The latest computer virus can gobble up the latest software in seconds; recession and slump can suddenly strike even the strongest economy

- **demanding** – both in terms of focus and allegiance. Jesus insists that we cannot be the servants of both God and *mammon* – an Aramaic word meaning 'the idol of wealth'

- **anxiety increasing** – again, perhaps surprisingly, Jesus does not teach that materialism will diminish our capacity for anxiety, but rather that it is likely to increase the futile habit of worry

- **disorientating** – a preoccupation with the material and the accompanying anxiety causes us to lose sight of our true value in the eyes of our God – are you not worth more than the birds? (Matt 6:26)

Not a new law of poverty

At least some of the disciples could be described as middle class::

- The father of James and John employed day labourers (Mark 1:20)

- Matthew, as a tax collector, would have been well off economically, albeit living a life on the fringe of society

- Some of the women who travelled with Jesus and the disciples were well-to-do (Luke 8:1–3)

- Jesus expected adult children to support their parents financially (Mark 7:9), thus implying the legitimacy of property

- Zacchaeus can retain a significant proportion of his possessions (Luke 10:8).

The list could be extended.

How can this evidence be squared with the criticism of the accumulation of property found in passages such as these?

- "You cannot serve both God and Money." (Luke 16:13)

- "Blessed are you who are poor, for yours is the kingdom of God… But woe to you who are rich." (Luke 6:20, 24)

- "Sell everything you have and give to the poor." (Luke 18:22)

This selection, taken together with the previous evidence for the legitimacy of property, suffices to demonstrate that the question of

HERE COMES THE JUDGE?

What does Jesus mean? Surely what Jesus is attacking here is a judgmental attitude towards other people. He is warning that we must not judge harshly, condemning others with censorious and carping criticism. We are not to set ourselves up as God, and judge our fellow men and women when we are in no position to do so. We are not to magnify the errors and weaknesses of others and make the worst of them. We are not to be faultfinders who are negative and destructive towards other people and enjoy actively seeking out their failures. As Martyn Lloyd Jones put it: 'If we ever know the feeling of being rather pleased when we hear something unpleasant about another, that is the wrong spirit.'

We are not to have the self-righteous attitude of the Pharisees 'who were confident of their own righteousness and looked down on everybody else' (Luke 18:9), which Jesus illustrated with the parable of the Pharisee and the tax collector. We are not to despise others and regard them with contempt. This applies to all our fellow human beings, whether they are Christians or not. We are not to adopt a superior attitude of unqualified condemnation to those who are not Christians. As Christians, we have received mercy. We have Christ's righteousness, not our own, and so we have no cause for pride. We should not patronize non-Christians or, worse still, judge and condemn them. If this applies to those who are not Christians, how much more should it apply to our brother and sister.

– Nicky Gumbel

There is an ancient Greek legend about the god *Monas*. He had a reputation among the other gods for being a constant critic. One day the gods had a competition to see who could make something really special. One of them made a man – and Monas criticised it because it didn't have a window in the front so that he could see what the man was thinking. Another built a superb house – and Monas criticised it because it didn't have wheels so that it could be moved to another location. Another of the gods made a bull and Monas criticised it too; he said the horns should be below the eyes so that it could see what it was goring. And at the end of the competition Monas got the boot out of heaven! He was banished to a domain of his own where he could criticize himself as much as he wanted to.

– Stephen Gaukroger

King of the hill

"As we live from God and God's world, a beauty is ours that overwhelms the flowers. If God adorns the grasses that pass in a day, to be burned as fuel or as trash, will he not do much more for you? You little-faiths! (6:30). Here Jesus uses a term that may have been his own invention: *oligopistoi*, 'little-faiths.' It occurs ten times in five verses in the Gospels. It seems to have been a nickname that he invented as a way of gently chiding his apprentices for their lack of confidence in God and in himself."
– *Dallas Willard*

"I am not anxious about tomorrow because I have prayed today about tomorrow!"
– *Michael Eaton*

"Whenever the Gospel is taught and people seek to live according to it, there are two terrible plagues that always arise: false preachers who corrupt the teaching, and then Sir Greed, who obstructs right living."
– *Martin Luther*

"Descartes concluded that the gift of reason is central to what it means to be human – to think is to be. Sartre's existentialism placed a new emphasis on self-assertion through action – to do is to be. As the twentieth century comes to an end, the great cities of the Western world demonstrate a new centre to our sense of identity – to shop is to be, *Tesco ergo sum*."
– *Rob Warner*

wealth and poverty cannot be reduced to one universal rule. Jesus pointed people in a variety of directions regarding money and possessions, so his instruction to one person cannot be interpreted as a universal law for all.

Though not evil in itself, material wealth can easily be counterproductive to the values or impact of the gospel. Where that is the case, its radical disposal in favour of the needy can become necessary.

Pause button
Do you own your possessions, or do they own you? If you lost all your possessions and investments overnight, what difference would it make? Do they all belong to God? Could you say, with Job; "The Lord gave and the Lord has taken away; may the name of the Lord be praised."

Friends of the King: his friends are our friends Matt 6:12–15, 7:1–5

Our spirituality must affect our lifestyle and the value systems we base it upon – and now we move on to see that spirituality is also going to affect the way that we relate to each other. This is very important – we have all met 'spiritual' Christians who profess to love God but can't stand people. They know the mechanics and disciplines of prayer (or so they think) but continue to gossip, criticize and be generally anything but Christ-like in their behaviour outside of their devotional life.

The King's friends will forgive (6:12–15)
A genuine spiritual life continually alerts us to our ongoing need of the Father's forgiveness – and our ongoing need to forgive others. The Bible does not paint the life of fellowship as an unreal utopia. It understands that we need to forgive each other and put up with each other too (Col 3:13). Forgiveness is based in the will (we choose) and not our feelings.

Unforgiveness:
● is contagious – bitterness spreads quickly
● holds us in our past – we are captive to the events of yesterday

THE KING'S FRIENDSHIP

PEARLS BEFORE SWINE

"Do not give to dogs what is holy, and do not throw your pearls before pigs. If you do they will trample them down with their feet and turn to attack you." (Matt 7:6) The phraseology is probably *chiastic* (that is, having an A-B-B-A structure). It can be translated:

A   Do not give to dogs what is holy,

B   and do not throw your pearls before pigs.

B   If you do the pigs will trample down the pearls with their feet

A   and the dogs will turn to attack you.

It is often said that the Sermon on the Mount consists of random sayings strung together loosely. Actually, there is logical sequence and development all the way through the Sermon on the Mount. Matt 7:6 is the only verse where there is at first some difficulty seeing where it fits in. It goes on to a slightly different point but one closely connected to verses 1–5. Verses 1–5 have to do with judging fellow disciples. Now verse 6 goes on to deal with what is likely to happen if the hypocritical disciple tries to impose his perfectionism on outsiders.

A fellow disciple is likely to judge us in the way we judge him. An outsider will be more aggressive altogether. Let the hypocritical disciple try to impose his inconsistent and hypocritical criticism on the 'dogs and pigs' who have no interest in living a godly life anyway, and see what response he will get! His pearls of moral analysis will be trodden down with scorn, and his offers of help with the speck of dust will be received with violent indignation. 'Who are you to turn to me with your advice? What about this ... and that ... and this ... in your life? The pigs and dogs of this world – who do indeed need help – have no time for the Christian with an obvious plank of wood in his eye. 'What is holy' refers to the gospel.

This is the most searching, challenging and humbling part of the Sermon on the Mount, especially for preachers and theologians and moral analysts! How easily self-righteousness grips us. How much criticism and how little appreciation! Self-righteousness exposes all things, is sceptical of all things, is suspicious of all things, slanders all things, and endures nothing! It criticizes specks and tolerates logs. It speaks when it has no right to speak. It interferes when the matter has nothing to do with us. It gets irritated with people easily and denounces them.

– Michael Eaton

King
of the hill

> "'Judge' is being used here in the sense of 'condemn' or 'pass final judgment as if we were God'. We are not to act as if we are God. 'It is mine to avenge,' says God (Rom 12:19). 'Judge nothing before the time,' says Paul. God is the searcher of hearts. He – and he alone – is capable of fully assessing genuineness and integrity. Our opinions are at best provisional."
>
> *– Michael Eaton*

> "It is preoccupation with possessions more than anything else that prevents men from living freely and nobly."
>
> *– Bertrand Russell*

> "If it don't make money, it ain't pretty."
>
> *– a Texas millionaire*

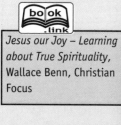

Jesus our Joy – Learning about True Spirituality, Wallace Benn, Christian Focus

- can be passed on as a second-hand item. It is easy to pick up the offences of others – particularly in local church life, where we are committed to care about each other's concerns
- can lead us into the practice of false judgment.

Here comes the judge?

The command of Jesus, "Do not judge, or you too will be judged" (Matt 7:1) is probably one of the most frequently misused quotations in history. It is clear, as we compare scripture with scripture, that certain types of judgment are our responsibility:

- State authorities have a God-given mandate to provide justice and therefore judgment (Rom 13:4). Tolstoy was wrong in his belief that Christ "forbade any form of law court."
- Parents have a responsibility for the nurture and discipline of their children – requiring judgment. (Eph 6:4)
- church leaders have a responsibility for church discipline (1 Cor 5:3, 12–13; 2 Tim 4:2)
- False teaching should be judged and discerned (Gal 1:8–9, 2:11, 5:12)
- We have a responsibility to judge whether someone is caught in sin: "if someone is caught in a sin, you who are spiritual should restore him gently" (Gal 6:1)

The judgment that Jesus condemns is the unjust, reactionary, hyper-critical attitude that is based on pride and arrogance rather than the love of God. Such an attitude will:

- bring judgment upon us. Our severity brings upon us God's severity. If we claim to be 'teachers' in our censorious attitudes we get more severe judgment from God (see James 3:1)
- be inconsistent. The "plank in your own eye" teaching shows us how diligent we can about other people's lives and how strangely and deceptively tolerant we can be about our own
- be counter-productive. Jesus wants us to be able to help one another and even confront each other – but that should be done in the attitude of humility that comes when we are quick to deal with our own sins first
- be inflammatory – one commentator interprets the advice not to give "pearls to pigs … [they may] tear you to pieces" as describing what will happen when the judgmental, critical disciple tries to inflict judgment on an outsider.

THE KING'S FRIENDSHIP

THEO LINK

PEARLS

Do not give dogs what is holy, and do not throw your pearls before swine, lest they [the swine] trample them underfoot and [the dogs] turn to attack you (Matt 7:6).

The construction of this saying seems to be *chiastic*. It is the swine that will trample the pearls beneath their feet and the dogs that will turn and bite the hand that fed them, even if it fed them with 'holy' flesh.

The general sense of the saying is clear. Objects of value, special privileges, participation in sacred things should not be offered to those who are incapable of appreciating them. Pearls are things of beauty and value to many people – Jesus himself in one of his parables compared the kingdom of God to a 'pearl of great price' (Matt 13:45–46) – but pigs will despise them because they cannot eat them. Holy flesh – the flesh of sacrificial animals – has a religious value over and above its nutritive value for worshippers who share in a 'peace offering' but pariah dogs will make no difference between it and scraps of offal for which they battle in the street; they win not feel specially grateful to anyone who gives it to them.

But has the saying a more specific application? One could imagine its being quoted by some more restrictive brethren in the Jerusalem church as an argument against presenting the gospel to Gentiles, certainly against receiving them into full Christian fellowship. At a slightly later date it was used as an argument against admitting unbelievers to the Lord's Supper.

Thus the *Didache* (Teaching of the Twelve Apostles), a manual of Syrian Christianity dated around AD100, says: "Let none eat or drink of your Eucharist except those who have been baptised in the name of the Lord. It was concerning this that the Lord said, 'Do not give dogs what is holy.'" It would be anachronistic to read this interpretation back into the ministry of Jesus. It is better to read the saying in the context given it by Matthew (the only Gospel writer to report it). It comes immediately after the injunction, 'Judge not, that you be not judged' (Matt 7:1), with two amplifications of that injunction: you will be judged by the standard you apply in the judgment of others (7:2); and you should not try to remove a speck of sawdust from someone else's eye when you have a whole plank in your own (7:3–5). Then comes this saying, which is a further amplification of the principle, or rather a corrective of it: you must not sit in judgment on others and pass censorious sentences on them, but you ought to exercise discrimination. Judgment is an ambiguous word, in English as in Greek: it may mean sitting in judgment on people (or even condemning them), or it may mean exercising a proper discrimination. In the former sense judgment is deprecated; in the latter sense it is recommended. Jesus himself knew that it was useless to impart his message to some people: he had no answer for Herod Antipas when Herod 'questioned him at some length' (Luke 23:9).

– FF Bruce

King *of the hill*

"Get a friend to tell you your faults, or better still welcome an enemy who will watch you keenly and sting you savagely. What a blessing such an irritating critic will be to a wise man, what an intolerable nuisance to a fool! Correct yourself diligently and frequently, or you will fall into errors unawares, false tones will grow, and slovenly habits will form insensibly; therefore criticise yourself with unceasing care."

– *Charles Haddon Spurgeon*

Studies in the Sermon on the Mount, Oswald Chambers, OCP

Friends of the King: loyally obeying him and walking with him until the end Matt 7:6–29

As our look at the Great Sermon draws to an end, we must avoid the temptation to walk away from the zones with an expanded understanding and a Study Guide full of jottings and notes – and little more.

The King of the Hill invites us to **do** what he says, with his strength at work within us, helping us along – then we shall be like those who build their houses upon the rock.

We need to keep going, through good times and bad, through success and failure, through times of great faith, and times when God seems distant.

Today we have seen that the King calls us to:

● **Keep on asking** – the command that we ask, seek, and knock in prayer suggests both perseverance and increasing intensity in our requests. 'Those that don't ask, don't have' is a maxim that applies to prayer and friendship with Jesus (James 4:2)

● **Keep remembering** that our God is both Father and friend. We hold before us a picture of the Father who is the very best parent that there has ever been, and who loves to give good gifts to his children – this is the vision that calls us to engage in daily friendship and intimacy with him.

● **Keep on doing good**. The golden rule that Jesus taught is the summary of the Great Sermon – as Luther said, "[Jesus] wraps up in a little package where all can be found". This rule of thumb is the key to unlock a thousand moral dilemmas.

● **Keep choosing the right way**. The teaching about gates and paths is not about entering the kingdom in terms of becoming a Christian, but rather entering into the fullness of life that the kingdom offers now. To continue to live the life of the kingdom, we have to make good decisions on a daily basis.

● **Keep your guard** against false teaching and false prophets, who will be disguised but can be known by their fruits (what they produce in character and conduct), their teaching (the words they speak) and their motives (money – they are greedy wolves – though some commentators suggest that their 'greed' is to attack the flock of God).

● **Keep living and doing** and not just believing. The King's friends are not saved because of their good works, but because of their salvation they do good works.

ENTIRELY SOVEREIGN?

God's response to our prayers is not a charade. He does not pretend that he is answering our prayer when he is only doing what he was going to do anyway. Our requests really do make a difference in what God does or does not do. The idea that everything would happen exactly as it does regardless of whether we pray or not is a spectre that haunts the minds of many who sincerely profess belief in God. It makes prayer psychologically impossible, replacing it with dead ritual at best. And of course God does not respond to this. You wouldn't either.

Suppose your children believed that you never did anything differently because they asked you. For example, you will give them money on Friday evening regardless of whether they ask you for it or not. But they also believe that you require them to go through the ritual of asking. And so they do it. On Friday evening they approach you and ask you to give them some weekend money. They do it even though they believe that you will or will not give it to them regardless of what they do, and that you know that they believe this. This, unfortunately, is the idea some people have of prayer.

Of course this is not the biblical idea of prayer, nor is it the idea of people for whom prayer is a vital part of life.

God can be prevailed upon by those who faithfully stand before him. We should recall here our earlier discussion of how parents respond to the requests of their children. There is nothing automatic about requests. There is no 'silver bullet' in prayer. Requests may be granted. Or they may not. Either way, it will be for a good reason. That is how relationships between persons are, or should be.

God is great enough that he can conduct his affairs in this way. His nature, identity, and overarching purposes are no doubt unchanging. But his intentions with regard to many particular matters that concern individual human beings are not. This does not diminish him. Far from it. He would be a lesser God if he could not change his intentions when he thinks it is appropriate. And if he chooses to deal with humanity in such a way that he will occasionally think it appropriate, that is just fine.

– *Adapted from* The Divine Conspiracy, *Dallas Willard*

King
of the hill

"Confucius, for example, is credited with having said, 'Do not to others what you would not wish done to yourself;' and the Stoics had an almost identical maxim. In the Old Testament Apocrypha we find: 'Do not do to anyone what you yourself would hate,' and this, it seems, is what the famous Rabbi Hillel quoted in circa 20BC when asked by a would-be proselyte to teach him the whole law while standing on one leg. His rival Rabbi Shammai had been unable or unwilling to answer, and had driven the enquirer away, but Rabbi Hillel said: 'What is hateful to you, do not do to anyone else. This is the whole law – all the rest is only commentary.'"

– John Stott

"Sound doctrine and holy living are the marks of true prophets."

– J.C. Ryle

THE LAST WORD

Over the last four days we have seen that the King opens his arms, calling us to a radically different lifestyle – where nothing about us is outside of the sphere of his rule.

We have asked searching questions about the true nature of success and hear the King's counsel that true success is found as we pursue his kingdom with single-minded determination. Life with the King of the hill demands that we adopt his priorities – for the last, the least and the lost. Some of the King's family around the world are currently in prison or facing death because they have made his priorities their own.

We have been called to a kingdom community, a working model on display for all to see. Citizens of that community will have the distinctive hallmark of the King's presence in every area of their lives.

Finally, none of this is remotely possible without the King's friendship. Without him, we can do nothing (John 15:5). Without Jesus as the source and centre of our lives, the Sermon on the Mount towers over us as a lofty and unattainable ideal.

For the crowds that stood on the hillside to listen to Jesus, the Sermon ended – and many of them followed Jesus, the King of the Hill, back down the mountainside and for a while, into the next adventure (Matt 8:1).

Will we do the same?

Be Thou my Vision, O Lord of my heart;
Naught be all else to me, save that Thou art
Thou my best thought, by day or by night,
Waking or sleeping, Thy presence my light.

Be Thou my Wisdom, Thou my true Word;
I ever with Thee, Thou with me, Lord;
Thou my great Father, I thy true son;
Thou in me dwelling, and I with Thee one.

Be Thou my battle shield, sword for the fight;
Be Thou my dignity, Thou my delight,
Thou my soul's shelter, Thou my high tower:
Raise Thou me heavenward, O Power of my power.

Riches I heed not, nor man's empty praise;
Thou mine inheritance, now and always:
Thou and Thou only, first in my heart,
High King of heaven, my treasure Thou art.

High King of heaven, after victory won,
May I reach heav'n's joys, O bright heaven's Sun!
Heart of my own heart, whatever befall,
Still be my Vision, O Ruler of all.

– Ancient Irish hymn, tr. E.H. Hull (1860–1935)
versified by M.E. Byrne (1880–1931)

NOTES

NOTES

King
of the hill

NOTES